The Adoption Book

also by Sheila Macmanus
published by Paulist Press

COMMUNITY ACTION SOURCEBOOK:
EMPOWERMENT OF PEOPLE

Sheila Macmanus

THE ADOPTION BOOK

PAULIST PRESS ◇ NEW YORK ◇ RAMSEY

Library of Congress
Catalog Card Number: 83-62018

ISBN: 0-8091-2578-1

Published by Paulist Press
545 Island Road, Ramsey, N.J. 07446

Printed and bound in the
United States of America

Contents

Contents

Acknowledgments

I particularly wish to thank those adoptive parents who took the time to respond to my questionnaire. Most preferred to remain anonymous. Out of respect for their privacy I totally changed all descriptive comments when reporting what "one adoptive parent . . ." said. The ideas presented do reflect the thoughts of adoptive parents either queried or shared with me over time, but the brief descriptions are fictitious.

I also keenly appreciate those wonderful state level child welfare "bureaucrats" who responded so promptly to my query, and the staffs of the many agencies and organizations I contacted, most of which are mentioned in this book, who shared their perspectives on adoption with me and who provided such a wealth of material about what they were doing, how, and why. For those agencies and groups profiled in the book I took great care to represent them accurately, using in the profiles their own words if at all possible. Thank you all for your support of this work.

Finally, I wish to thank my great cheerleaders—Matt, Nathaniel, and Adam, three of the hottest resources around.

To my children,
Matthew, Nathaniel, and Adam, and to Vera Thomas—
living proof that brotherhood and motherhood
extend beyond all flesh

INTRODUCTION

This book is written for people who wish to adopt and for others who wish to support adoption—in short, all those who wish to contribute in some way to giving children the "chance of a lifetime." Although the book is not written for professionals in the adoption field, I hope the psychological and sociological insights will be thought-provoking for professionals and lay persons alike.

In our times the emphasis in adoption is not finding children for childless couples, but rather finding loving permanent families for homeless children.

To serve this purpose, this book is divided into four chapters. The first is an adoption overview and includes suggested perspectives on adoption and homeless children, some historical information, some statistics, and a forward look.

Chapter II deals with some key adoption issues—baby selling, independent (non-agency) adoption, open adoption, sealed records, single parent adoption, transracial and mixed race adoption—in a question and answer format. Over the years I have been asked many questions about these issues; I attempted to find and present the best answers available, of course according to my own lights. In these answers and in the commentary throughout the book I have also incorporated the responses of the adoptive parents who responded to my questionnaire.

Chapter III is a resource chapter. It is divided into four sections. Special Needs Adoption is first and longest because it is most important; these are the waiting children. Then follow sections on Intercountry Adoption, Public and Licensed Private Agency Adoption in general, and National and

1

Local Advocates/Support Groups. Each of these sections has three parts: Remarks, Profiles, and Resources. Remarks and Resources are self-explanatory. As to Profiles, the Special Needs section, for example, profiles some excellent agencies and exchanges active in the placement of special needs kids. Each profile contains a portion on "What You Can Do To Help."

Chapter IV contains a discussion of Federal/Corporate/State activity in relation to adoption. The last portion of this chapter consists of a table of basic state adoption information—who can adopt, who can be adopted, etc.—based on a primary research query I conducted of the fifty states, the District of Columbia, Puerto Rico and Guam. Of the fifty-three governments involved, forty-five responded with descriptions of their adoption statutes and practices. Some of the attitudes reflected in the responses of these public child welfare professionals have been incorporated into commentary in various portions of the book.

The Appendix contains the United Nations *Draft Declaration on Social and Legal Principles Relating to the Protection and Welfare of Children, with Special Reference to Foster Placement and Adoption Nationally and Internationally.* The Appendix also includes a bibliography of some of the fine books and material available on the general subject of adoption, most of which are not mentioned elsewhere in the book. The first portion of this list consists of books written about the personal experiences of adoptive families and children. These are of the case study and personal narrative variety, very readable and informative in that special way that a resource book such as this cannot be. Lastly I have included an alphabetized address list of all the addresses contained in the book and then some.

Two final notes. This book does not speak to specific adoption policy issues which are currently being debated by professionals in the field. Policy matters are touched on throughout the book, and are addressed specifically in Chapter IV and in the above mentioned *United Nations Declaration.*

The book also does not deal with making the decision to adopt, although in the Special Needs: Remarks section there is some food for thought in this regard.

I.

Adoption Overview

"How many wonders you have done for us,
   Yahweh, my God!
How many plans you have made for us;
   you have no equal!"

—Psalm 40:5

Personal Perspectives, Ethics, and Common Sense

> "Liberty, Equality, Fraternity, or Death—the last, much the easiest to bestow . . ."
> —Charles Dickens, *A Tale of Two Cities*

Adopting a child is not easy. Once a child is adopted, adoptive parenting is difficult and rewarding—just as biological parenting is difficult and rewarding. Both demand taking loving responsibility for children God has assigned to us before time began.

The challenges unique to adoptive parenting have been enlarged by conventional attitudes. Some of the most enlightened persons in our culture continue to ask a parent of both biological and adopted offspring: "Which of these are your *real* children?" Others tell a couple who recently adopted their first child, "It's so good of you to raise *someone else*'s child; too bad you couldn't have one of your *own.*"

Excellent adoption advocacy groups and agencies in the forefront of facilitating adoptions in our country still refer to the birth parents as the "natural" parents, when in reality the birth parents are the birth parents and the adoptive parents are the "natural" parents.

One older adoptive mother told me: "Early on we told our daughter: 'A very nice lady grew you in her uterus for us.' As she grew older we used the phrase 'biological mother' in reference to the nice lady and always 'real mother' in relation to myself."

I recall a picture in *Newsweek* magazine several years ago, the caption of which amazed me. It was a picture of actress Mia Farrow and four of her children. The caption carefully distinguished between her biological children and her adopted children, but not in those terms. It was on the order of "Mia Farrow with her two children and her two adopted children." Do we

5

have so limited a sense of parenthood and what it involves? Do we have so little faith in the prescience of God in drawing up the list of families?

For Christians and multitudes of others on our planet who converse daily with a God who knows their names, adoption should perhaps mean that a child who was given a name in pre-time has after a time found the family with the same name(s).

This is the reason why using the phrase "we chose you" might be inappropriate in speaking to your adopted child. A single man who adopted an older institutionalized child told his son, "God made up the lists of families. God told me how to find you. Isn't that exciting?"

For an older adopted child who knew his birth parents, who may have lived the first ten years of his life with them, the words may vary but the spirit remains the same. To any adopted child, to any child, permanence and security should be the order of the day, with a healthy respect for the validity of the experiences that came before the finding of the child's "forever family."

Those of us who believe in the Word before time began and those of us who believe in the parenthood of God must very naturally take to the deepest and richest understanding of parenthood, and therefore of adoption.

(All of this does not negate the fact that if two of my three children when grown wish to locate their birth parents I will lend them *every* assistance in their search. While children are minors they live for the most part with parental definitions; when they are older they will define adoption and parenthood for themselves.)

The very existence of articles about "when to tell" your child he or she is adopted reflects society's tenacious discomfort with adoption. (The author of one book I examined in my research actually suggests that the adoptive parents tell as few people as possible about the adoption in an effort to *never* tell the child he or she is adopted! This book was written in 1971 and was the singular exception to the rule.)

One fine commentator on adoption cites "erroneous ideas about blood ties" as one of several motives that account for the persistence of less than positive reactions to adoption in our times. (The other motives: "the survival of Roman law, pseudo-religious morals, family and social convention, fear of heredity, fear of the mother's return and fear of scandal, and, above all, losing sight of the priority interests involved, that is to say the interests of the child, which are all too often sacrificed to a number of interests of secondary importance.")[1]

It seems that blood ties still count most in our society. We have an *unnatural* attachment to whose sperm and whose ovum made the child. In determining priorities for foster care children this helps—our first priority is the return of the child to his or her birth parents if in the child's best interest. It runs against us when it is determined that that same child's real parents should be his adoptive parents.

As most parents will tell you, parenthood is validated not by conception and delivery, which dogs, pigs, and squirrels do all the time, but by upkeep in all senses of the word. The real parent offers the child a secure and loving family and takes care of his or her most basic needs. As another adoptive mother put rather bluntly to me: "The real parent is the parent who teaches them to wipe themselves and who wipes them in the meantime."

Psychologists point to the real parent as the parent who engages with the child in the "bonding" process. In their 1973 book, *Beyond the Best Interests of the Child,* Solnit, Goldstein, and Freud

> argued that the child's "real" parent is the one with whom he or she establishes a bond, the "psychological" parent who is supportive on a day-to-day basis. "The child's best interests," says Solnit, "require a guiding, protective parent who wants him and gives him a feeling of being wanted."[2]

Security is what we must give to children to do "right" and good by them. "Social workers say that if a child has a secure family, he doesn't need much else, and without that, it doesn't matter what else he has."[3]

The need for the security of a family and one set of parents came home to me in an interview I had with a birth parent. The interview was actually connected to the issue of independent adoption but was fruitful in several respects.

The young woman had given birth to a child out of wedlock and had decided to transfer parental rights and responsibilities. The adoption was arranged privately through an attorney. The young woman knows the city in which the child, now five years old, lives. It became clear to me that, although always feeling loving concern for the child, over the past five years she had been *most* interested in a tangible connection to the child when her own fortunes, her own personal relationships were lowest. She told me of her deep desire at this point to have a picture of the little girl. She had recently contacted her lawyer with this request who then contacted the lawyer of the adoptive parents. The parents' response was negative. The young woman was disappointed.

Having an adopted child of the same age, I shared with her what I thought their perspectives might be. I told her that the child she had given life to needed most the security that she had found with one set of parents. At the least they probably did not think that their five year old needed to be confused by the appearance of her birth parent (for how were they to know what the photo would lead to). I told her that my response would have been the same. "My five year old doesn't need that kind of confusion," I said. "When he is twenty-five the story will be different and it will be up to him what kind and how many relationships he maintains in his life." I also told her that she may well have a long life of friendship and closeness with the girl after she reaches adulthood—a phase all parents look forward to and increasing numbers of birth parents are choosing to experience.

The need for security and a permanent plan for those children waiting in foster care is high on any list of what is good for our children and our world. The United Nations declaration concerning the welfare of children (see Appendix) sees foster care as temporary, as a "bridge to permanence." And another commentator tells us:

> Foster care is, or should be, for the child that needs a home for six months or less, while his folks are getting it together or the department gets it apart, legally, so that he has as much permanency in his life as soon as possible. When (and it should be in rare cases) children are in foster care over a year, the foster parents should be the first to be considered in an adoption, not because there are no other adoptive families available, but because it is less traumatic for the child.[4]

It should disturb us that of the approximately one half million children now in foster care, one in four have been in care more than *six years*![5]

The courts are supporting the idea of permanency and security for children more and more. Joan McNamara in her fine book *The Adoption Adviser* cites the example of the courts awarding custody to foster parents when after nine years with them the biological mother wanted custody. The courts serve as the voice of the child in these cases.

Ideally, the essential elements of the legal framework of adoption are: the legal separation of the child from his birth parents, the transfer of custody to a qualified social agency, and the transfer of parental rights and responsibilities to the adoptive parents.[6] In all of this the child should have the preeminent position because the child is indeed the only person involved with no voice, no choice.

Because the children are so important, the symbols we use relative to adoption are important. The words of an adoption decree and the words spoken by the judge as he transfers parental rights and responsibilities are breathtaking; ask any adoptive parent. Over the course of history we have been sloppy in both our attitudes and our language concerning adoption and parenthood. It is now our challenge to mold the symbols connected with adoption to fit the true needs of the children involved and our more mature view of adoption. It is very important that we put ideas and words like "abandon a child" or "give a child up (for adoption)" behind us as a civilization. It is time we stop asking "Which is your *real* child?" It is time we celebrate the true meanings of parenthood, brotherhood, sisterhood and family by toasting our children with caring words, laws, and attitudes.

History

Adoption was prevalent among the ancient Greeks, Romans, Babylonians and Assyrians. The reason for adoption in ancient times was usually to provide an heir.

The Babylonian Code of Hammurabi of the eighteenth century B.C. includes a lengthy section concerning adoption. The Justinian Code of the sixth century A.D. also deals with it.

In our times adoption in the English speaking world is a recent addition to the legal codes which "has made its way against a belief in the absolute primacy of the biological link between parents and children. In English Common Law, parental rights and duties were traditionally inalienable—the first (English) Adoption Act was passed only in 1926."[7]

And in our own country, the first "jurisdiction to enact an adoption statute was Massachusetts—in 1851. Prior to this, as well as later in many jurisdictions, adoptions were negotiated by deed—a now obsolete practice."[8]

For a fine comprehensive treatment of the history of adoption see Mary Kathleen Benet's book, *The Politics of Adoption,* chapters 2 and 3.

Statistics

In this book we are talking about "non-relative" adoptions, that is, adoptions by people unrelated to the adoptee. Approximately one-half of current adoptions are by stepparents or relatives of orphans. We are here dealing with the other half.

Although the last statistics by the Department of Health and Human Services relative to adoption were collected for 1975, it is safe to estimate that there are roughly 100,000 children adopted each year and that one-half of these kids are adopted by relatives.

Approximately 8.5 million Americans cannot have children by birth.[9] Yet there are only about 40,000 to 50,000 available babies.[10] Fifteen to twenty couples wait for every healthy infant available. The wait for an infant may be many years, often long enough to put the couple over the eligible age limit.

Roughly a half million children are now in foster care, either waiting to be returned to their birth parents, or awaiting adoption. Those who are free to be adopted number probably between 100,000 and 125,000.[11]

The crucial question we must ask is: What about all these kids living the temporary lives of foster care? What can we do to assist in providing a plan for permanence for each of these children as soon as possible, as each year thousands more children flow into the foster care system? And what can we do to support the efforts of agencies and other groups to place the 100,000 foster kids who are already legally free to be adopted? Read on.

Looking Ahead

Many worthwhile ideas are coming out of the child welfare profession and from the pens of human behaviorists.

In special needs adoptions we need to support the idea of follow-up respite care. Not a new idea, respite care is a concept needing renewed interest and support. It gives the family of a developmentally or emotionally disabled child a necessary temporary break from their responsibilities. If you are not in a position to adopt such a special child, perhaps your family could regularly offer a day or weekend of respite care to a family who does adopt.

Since we are all living longer, how about those of grandparent age adopting special needs kids? Perhaps couples and individuals who are forty-five to fifty years of age and in good health could adopt a child who would otherwise remain in foster care or in an institution.

In the cause of parental bonding, a few hospitals have begun admitting the adoptive mother (why not father also?) to the maternity floor where she feeds the baby and keeps it in her room while the birth mother goes to another part of the hospital after delivery.

A fine call is being made to expand opportunities for adoption through community involvement and support. Good ideas now in various stages of implementation include active recruitment of adoptive homes, subsidies, review of adoption and child welfare legislation nationwide, adoption resource exchanges, and registries to facilitate reunions of adult adoptees and birth parents.

In the cause of giving more children the "chance of a lifetime," Robert Freitas writes about the prospect of fetal adoption and gives us food for thought:

> Progress at the forefront of current medical research suggests that human fetal transplantation and fullterm *in vitro* gestation may become technologically feasible by the end of the 1980s. Assuming these techniques are available, unwillingly pregnant women have an alternative to feticide or unwanted childbirth. The reluctant mother simply visits the local Fetal Adoption Center, undergoes surgery for removal of her viable fetus, signs

11

legal documents, and exits a free woman. At the same time, the developing embryo is preserved. Fetuses removed during the first trimester are transplanted into the uterus of a surrogate or infertile adoptive mother and carried to term in the usual manner. Second trimester fetuses are nurtured in warm, organic artificial wombs until the third trimester, when conventional modern incubation techniques can be brought into play. Fetuses taken during the third trimester are transferred directly to the incubator, an existing medical technology often used to save the lives of infants born up to three months premature.[12]

The Holt Agency (see Intercountry Adoption: Profiles) sums up the best and most ethical perspective on adoption: "Every child, of whatever nationality or race, has the right to grow up with parents of his own."

In Conclusion

The Christian base of adoption is more the parenthood of God than the brotherhood of man. (Adoption professionals say that if you think you are doing a child a favor or making a "sacrifice" by adopting, don't.) The deepest Christian perspective sees faith as work, sees challenges not as "difficult *but* rewarding" but as "difficult *and* rewarding."

Our children, whether biological or adopted, are on loan to us as special challenges, special gifts. In a very real sense adopted children are doing an eternal favor to the millions of childless couples and individuals who wait in anguish to be so blessed.

A couple and their three year old son were in an elevator ascending to the adoption office where they would pick up their new son and brother. The three year old was asked to lead a quick prayer. They joined hands and he said the only formal prayer he knew: "Bless us, O Lord, and these thy gifts, which we are about to receive . . ."

II.

Adoption Issues

"His mother and his brothers came looking for him, but they could not get to him because of the crowd. He was told, 'Your mother and brothers are standing outside and want to see you.' But he said in answer, 'My mother and my brothers are those who hear the word of God and put it into practice.'"

—Luke 8:19–21

Several issues related to the adoption process are more or less hotly discussed by prospective adoptive parents, adoptees, child welfare professionals and others. Among these are baby selling, independent adoption, open adoption, sealed records, single parent adoption, and transracial and mixed race adoption.

In the last decade millions of children have not made it into the world to be adopted. The effect has been the rise of illegal adoptions or technically legal but immoral adoptions, that is, baby selling. Other waiting parents have turned in large numbers to independent adoptions. Instead of going through the lengthy and sometimes fruitless process of licensed agency adoption they turn to their family doctor or lawyer who "knows someone" who is "in trouble."

In recent times biological and adoptive parents are experimenting with the idea of open adoption, that is, having more information available to adoptive parents at the outset and in some cases having continuing contact between the biological and adoptive parents. In turn, many already adopted children have found that in the age of "freedom of information" they should have access to knowledge of their biological forebears. Enter the sealed records issue.

With a larger percentage of our children being brought up in single parent homes, the idea of single parenthood has gained currency in our society and the reality of single parenthood is no longer the exception. Single persons who have wished to be parents are now taking steps to realize their hopes.

A final topic which is treated in the following pages and which has been a focus of controversy in the last several years is the issue of transracial and mixed race adoption. Should parents of one race adopt a child of another race? What about children of more than one race—where do they belong?

The following section asks and answers the most frequently raised questions about these issues.

BABY SELLING

Q When does an independent (legal) adoption become baby selling?

A People are not allowed under law to sell their children. It *is* legal for a parent to pay an attorney to assist in transferring parental rights. The process becomes technically illegal when money passes hands to actually pay for the baby. However, there are ways of disguising the payment.

Q How is the process of baby selling different from regular independent adoptions?

A "Most of the time the process of baby selling is the same as that of legal independent placements, but the payments made for the birth mother's expenses and the legal fees are so high that it is obvious the baby is being sold."[1]

Q How many babies are "sold" each year?

A "An estimated 5,000 to 10,000 babies are given up in high price adoptions facilitated by attorneys and physicians each year (representing one-fourth of all non-relative adoptions and one-half of all private non-relative adoptions)."[2]

16

Q How much does a black market adoption cost?

A A white adoption can cost anywhere from $4,000 to $40,000 or more. "It's a seller's market right now," explains one lawyer, whose fees for such adoptions range from $7,000 to $9,000, not including medical and other expenses.[3]

Q Who are the people who deal in babies?

A "Those in the white-baby adoption business are no longer state-certified social workers and government or religious agencies, but a small group of private entrepreneurs, dealers, and middlemen who have turned a placement into a deal. Suitable couples are not sought for homeless children; couples shop for suitable children—those of the best stock with the best physical and mental characteristics and the least likelihood of being defective . . . the only criterion for a couple's suitability is ability to pay."[4]

Q What is a good resource on the subject?

A Lynne McTaggart's book, *The Baby Brokers: The Marketing of White Babies in America,* Dial Press, 1980.

INDEPENDENT ADOPTIONS

Q What is an "independent" adoption?

A An independent adoption is one handled without a licensed agency as an intermediary. In most cases the birth parent surrenders parental rights to an adoptive couple with an attorney or a doctor as facilitator.

Q Are many children adopted independently?

A "Nationwide estimates show that independent placements exceed agency placements two-to-one."[1]

Q Why do so many birth mothers choose independent adoptions?

A • They may be uninformed about available agency services.
• They may desire to avoid telling others about the pregnancy, others who might be involved if they went through an agency.
• In private adoptions the adoptive parents pay for medical expenses and other tangible services.
• They may wish to avoid the possibility of the child being in foster care after birth while an agency arranges placement.

Q Why do so many prospective adoptive couples choose independent adoption?

A • It is easier for an adoptive couple to qualify, as eligibility requirements are not as tight or are virtually non-existent.
   • There is a shortage of healthy white infants; the couple might find themselves way down on an agency's waiting list, or ineligible.
   • The wait for a baby is much shorter.

Q Why do so many child welfare professionals oppose the idea of independent adoptions?

A • The home study is frequently not as rigorous as that connected to an agency placement. A 1978 study reported:

"Only six states require an investigation of the home prior to the placement of a child. This means that in the vast majority of independent placements in this country, there is no assessment of the home by an authorized agent of the state prior to the placement. Although most states require a home study prior to the completion of an independent adoption, a few allow the investigation to be conducted by a 'disinterested person,' not necessarily someone trained to examine the adoptive couples' ability to provide for the child or the quality of care the child is receiving. Seventeen states allow waiver of the home study at the discretion of the court. Thus, under certain circumstances, there may be no scrutiny of the home."[2]

   • In most cases the birth parent does not receive any counseling about relinquishing her child.
   • In most cases the adoptive parents receive no counseling regarding why they want to adopt, what the challenges are, etc.
   • "A fairly large number of (the) interviews showed that the biological father's rights were either ignored or consciously denied."[3]
   • No provisions are made in case the adoptive couple changes their minds, for example, if the baby is born with a birth defect.

19

- There is the possibility of an unintended "open adoption" situation as the parties in private adoptions often are known to each other.

Q Are independent adoptions legal in all states?

A As of the end of 1981, private adoptions were legal in all states except Connecticut, Delaware, Massachusetts, Michigan, and Minnesota. Private placements made directly by the mother were allowed in fifteen states. The other states allowed them to be made by third parties, for example, doctors and lawyers.[4]

Q What are the state laws regarding adoption fees?

A As of 1978, ten states prohibited payment of compensation for placing a child. One-half of the states had no provision regarding fees or had provisions only applicable to agencies. At present, many states have no penalties or small penalties for violation of adoption statutes.[5]

Q What can be done legislatively?

A "Ideally, uniform regulatory legislation should extend equal protections to all adoptions. Absent the passage of the enlightened Model State Adoption Act, no nationwide uniformity in adoption law exists."[6]

Q Is adequate legislation enough?

A Child welfare professionals would say no: "Legislation can protect the child only if it is fortified by adequate social services, and . . . such services are best provided by organized agencies."[7]

Q If uniform national legislation is a long way off, should independent or private adoptions be outlawed across the board?

A Many child welfare professionals say yes. Others see alternatives: "There is evidence (in the study data) that some of the risks of independent adoptions are significantly diminished in the geographic areas where state laws and regulations are strong and specific, and where agency involvement in independent adoptions is mandated by law—Los Angeles and Iowa. In these areas, biological fathers are more likely to be involved; adoptive couples are more likely to have knowledge about the father's involvement; biological mothers are likely to perceive their relationships with the facilitators in a positive light; and adoptions are less likely to be judged legally questionable. It appears, then, that legislative and judicial reform, and the strengthening of the involvement of social agencies in the independent adoption process, can affect the nature of this process."[8]

Q What is a good resource on the subject?

A *Adoption Without Agencies* by Meezan, Katz, and Russo is a major study of independent adoptions. It can be ordered by contacting: The Child-Welfare League of America, Publications Service, 67 Irving Place, New York, New York 10003, 212-254-7410.

OPEN ADOPTION

Q What is open adoption?

A Open adoption really refers to an open placement process and the on-going contact between birth parents, adoptive parents and possibly the child which might result.

Q What happens in an open adoption?

A "In an open adoption, the birth parents meet the adoptive parents and participate in the separation and placement process. They relinquish all legal, moral, and nurturing rights to the child but retain the right to continuing contact and to knowledge of the child's whereabouts and welfare."[1]

Q Do agencies usually participate in open adoptions?

A Rarely. One exception is the Catholic Social Services agency in Green Bay, Wisconsin. This agency only places children if the adoptive parents are provided with full information about the child and that child's relatives. This information is primarily provided in writing. Often the adoptive and birth parents choose to meet each other. The agency helps with the original arrangements for such meetings but is not involved in any on-going contacts they may arrange except if asked to act as an intermediary for the future contacts.

Q Is it legal for this Catholic Social Services agency to use open records procedures?

A The open records procedures used by the Catholic Social Services agency in Green Bay, Wisconsin, *precede* the legal adoption, so at least in their state there is no legal barrier. "This option, insofar as we are aware, should be legal in other states, as most state statutes mandate closing records only after adoption has occurred."[2]

Q Why do so many child care professionals and others oppose the idea of open adoptions?

A Many professionals are concerned that the possibility of on-going contact with birth parents will be too confusing for the adopted child and will subtract significantly from the security he or she needs in having only one set of parents. A couple in the southwest who adopted a baby on the sudden death of his parents maintain contact with the boy's birth grandparents. They do not recommend such contact favorably. The contacts are confusing for the child and were even more so when he was younger. The couple has seen the need to set firm ground rules as to the frequency and the setup of the meetings. Child care professionals keenly see the possible pitfalls of on-going contact between birth parents and adoptive parents, although the great value of the adoptive parents having as much information as possible about the genetic, medical and social history of the child should not be underestimated. (See Issues: Sealed Records)

Q How might an open adoption process help children now waiting in foster care?

A "For many children—especially for those who remain in foster care because their parents cannot bear the idea of never seeing them again and thus do not terminate parental rights—it could be a step toward permanency."[3]

23

The Adoption Book

Q What is a good resource on the subject?

A Catholic Social Services in Green Bay has a kit available which explains their open adoption procedures. Enclose $15. Order from: Adoption Program Supervisor, Catholic Social Services, P.O. Box 38, Green Bay, Wisconsin 54305.

SEALED RECORDS

Q What is meant by "sealed records"?

A In most states adoption records are sealed or secured once a child is adopted. A new birth certificate is issued showing the names of the adoptive parents only. The sealed records can only be opened with a court order "based on 'good cause' which is generally not defined to include the simple desire to see one's own records."[1]

Q What is the history of sealed adoption records?

A The late Margaret Mead tells us, "The English passed their first laws regulating adoption in the 1920s, in response to the needs of war orphans of World War I. At that time they took over the practice of sealed records. But now, after some fifty years' experience, they have passed a new law that allows an 18 year old adoptee to sit down with a special counselor and learn the facts of her past."[2]

Q Why do many adult adoptees want to learn these facts?

A Many adoptees have simply experienced a strong desire to acknowledge blood ties. Some professionals see a value in the adoptee dealing in the reality of his or her past. "Recent researchers, notably Arthur Sorofsky and Annette Baran, point to the universality of the need for information about one's origins and to the damaging effects of secrecy. One of the most acutely painful effects of ignorance is the tendency to invest the unknown (birth) parents with too much importance, to fantasize about how their discovery will change the adoptee's life. If it does nothing else, a completed search will lay these fantasies to rest."[3] It is the strong belief of those searching for these origins that an adopted person over the age of eighteen (some say older) should be entitled to access to his or her original birth certificate.

Q That sounds like a reasonable request. What is all the controversy about?

A The decision to unseal birth records brings into conflict the birth mother's right to remain anonymous and the adult adoptee's right to information about the birth parents and himself or herself.

Q What is a possible solution to this conflict?

A "A compromise solution (might be) . . . boards of registry, to which both parties could make known their desire for information about each other. The boards would be able to trace and contact the parties separately, and could try to resolve conflicts where one party was reluctant to be identified or to have a reunion."[4]

Q Are there other alternatives to opening the birth records?

A Some groups advocate the transmission of non-identifying information at the outset of the adoption process: "what the ages of their biological parents were, what their nationality and religious preference were, whether they had diabetes or some other genetically significant health problem."[5]

Q What do the courts say?

A "The Supreme Court is clearly on the side of privacy, leaving decisions to open records or set up registries to the state legislatures."[6]

Q What are good resources on the subject?

A • You can order a copy of the model registry act, "An Act to Establish a Mutual Consent Voluntary Adoption Registry and to Provide for the Transmission of Nonidentifying Information on the Health History and the Genetic and Social History of Adoptees," by sending $2.20 to the National Committee for Adoption, 1346 Connecticut Avenue, N.W., Suite 326, Washington, D.C. 20036.
 • The Adoptees' Liberty Movement Association (ALMA) aims to establish free access to their records for eighteen year and older adoptees. For more information contact ALMA, P.O. Box 154, Washington Bridge Station, New York, New York 10033, 212-581-1568.

SINGLE PARENT ADOPTION

Q What is the history of single parent adoption in the United States?

A "In November of 1965, the Los Angeles County Department of Adoptions placed the first child in this country in a single-parent home, after the California State Department of Social Welfare had passed a regulation stating that 'single parent applications may be accepted only when a two-family home has not been found because of the child's special needs.' "[1]

Q Do any state laws prohibit adoption by single parents?

A "While no state law prohibits adoption by single parents, the California regulation is unique because it spells out what seems to be the tacit operating procedure among adoption agencies across the country," that is, single applicants are not discouraged but are low on the list of those waiting.[2]

Q In addition to the usual requirements, what are agencies most concerned about in single parent adoptions?

A Under special scrutiny with prospective single adoptive parents are the availability of a good support system, financial stability, and access to role models of the opposite sex.[3]

Q Are single parents less qualified for adoptive parenthood than married couples?

A Studies have shown singles by and large to be as qualified as married couples for adoptive parenthood. In fact, two researchers found that "with the increasing flexibility of contemporary sex roles, culturally appropriate role learning can be acquired from either parent as well as from both parents."[4]

Q Is it possible for single people to adopt children from other countries?

A "In . . . other countries a greater range of ages of children is available to American prospective parents. In Canada and Europe there are no children available. Adoption from the Middle East or other Moslem countries appears to face religious or legal restrictions. (There are) not yet sources in other African countries. In Latin America and Asia there are waiting children, although in some of these countries their own laws restrict or forbid adoption by single persons. However, international placement agencies, already overloaded with applications from couples, may be individually reluctant to accept applications from single U.S. citizens. The situation in Asia and Latin America is constantly changing, as countries revise their laws and policies governing inter-country adoption. Most of the Latin American countries which permit inter-country adoption require the prospective parents to travel to the country and stay there for one to six weeks while the legal adoption or transfer of custody takes place. Children available from Latin America usually have a mixture of Indian and Spanish in their background, with some black heritage on occasion."[5]

Q What are some good resources on the subject?

A • The Committee for Single Adoptive Parents, P.O. Box 4074, Washington, D.C. 20015 has membership services for single individuals including a Source List which cites agency or direct sources of adoptable children in the U.S. and abroad who will accept single applicants. The Committee also has available for $6.00 the *Handbook for Single Adoptive Parents.*

• "What It's Like For Singles Who Adopt: Four Family Stories," by Gini Kopecky, *MS* Magazine, June, 1977.

• "Single Parent Adoption" includes two articles. One, by researchers W. Feigleman and A. R. Silverman, reviews existing materials. The other is a personal essay by A. Richards which recounts what it is like to be a single adoptive parent. Order from LSDS, Dept. 76, Washington, D.C. 20401.

See the Intercountry Adoption: Resources section of this book for addresses of several groups which could be of assistance.

TRANSRACIAL AND MIXED RACE ADOPTION

Q What is transracial adoption?

A Transracial adoption is the adoption by parents of one race of a child of another race.

Q What is mixed race adoption?

A Mixed race adoption is adoption by parents of one race of a child of more than one (mixed) race.

Q Are most inter-racial adoptions of children of one race?

A With respect to blacks and whites, most inter-racial adoptions are of mixed race children, that is, they are *not transracial* adoptions.

Q What have been the objections raised by black social workers to the transracial adoption of black children by white families?

A   In 1972, the National Association of Black Social Workers issued the following statement: "We have taken the position that Black children should be placed only with Black families whether in foster care or for adoption. Black children belong physically, psychologically, and culturally in Black families in order that they receive the total sense of themselves and develop a sound projection of their future. Human beings are products of their environment and develop their sense of values, attitudes, and self-concept within their family structures. Black children in white homes are cut off from the healthy self-development of themselves as Black people."

Q   What has been the result of these objections?

A   Since that time a number of major agencies have been established for the purpose of placing black infants with black families. There has been an enormous effort including input of federal funds to support outreach to black communities to adopt black infants and older black children. Despite these efforts, "while no healthy black infant or small child waits long for a black family, there are older and handicapped minority children for whom families are still hard to find."[1]

Q   How many adoptable children are non-white?

A   "Authorities estimate that nearly 40 percent of the 125,000 adoptable children in the U.S. are non-white."[2]

Q   What do those adoptive parents feel who have adopted mixed race children?

A   Many feel that adoption of racially mixed children by either race involved should be encouraged. One couple I spoke with felt that the inclination to type a mixed race child as one or the other race was itself a form of racism. Both heritages or the several heritages involved should be acknowledged and appreciated in the most active and profound ways. The parents I contacted feel they are ahead of society on this point. While society catches up, they are trying by conscious choice of neighborhood, support group, etc., to take the brunt of living in the avant garde off the shoulders of their adopted children as much as is possible, while keeping in mind the true realities of the challenge. As one parent of a Native American/white child explained, "My daughter's birth mother was white, her birth father was Native American. She can lay equal claim to two heritages, two cultures, and a mix of physical attributes. This is the reality. She looks more Native American than white—does this mean she should feel less an identification with her birth mother and more with her birth father? On the other hand, if she could "pass" as white, should she ignore the heritage of her birth father? Parents who lack the energy and the imagination to encompass more than one heritage should not adopt children of mixed race."

Q What does the future hold?

A There will be a continuing increase of efforts to place single race children with families of their own race. With respect to mixed race children—whether adopted or the result of mixed marriages—the challenge to society to accept these children will remain. Since it will be impossible to find mixed race couples to match the racial mix of a given child, the challenge of a single race couple adopting a mixed race child will remain.

Q What are some good resources on the subject of transracial adoption?

A • "Children's Bureau Initiatives for the Adoption of Minority Children" outlines the various programs created under the Adoption Opportunities Program. Prepared by staff members of the Children's Bureau (DHHS), the monograph deals with the large population of minority

33

youngsters waiting to be adopted and special efforts being made to recruit black and minority families. Order #(OHDS) 81-30300 from LSDS, Dept. 76, Washington, D.C. 20401.

- "Finding Permanent Homes for Black Children: The California Inland Area Urban League Project," by Linda Dunn, *Children Today,* September/October, 1981. This article attributes the success of this project to (1) sponsorship of the Urban League, (2) an adoption specialist/advocate, (3) cooperation of county adoption agencies, (4) continuous involvement and support of an advisory committee. For more information about the project contact the National Urban League, 500 E. 62nd Street, New York, New York 10021.
- Anderson, *Children of Special Value: Interracial Adoption in America,* St. Martin's Press, 1971.
- Fanshel, *Far From the Reservation: The Transracial Adoption of American Indian Children,* Scarecrow Press, 1972.
- Grow and Shapiro, *Transracial Adoption Today: Views of Adoptive Parents and Social Workers,* Child Welfare League of America, 1975.

III.

Adoption Resources

"Ask and it will be given to you; search, and you will find; knock, and the door will be opened to you."

—Matthew 7:7

SPECIAL NEEDS ADOPTION: *Remarks*

Special needs children are variously defined. They include children who are waiting to be adopted who are older—some say over five, others say over nine—have physical or mental disabilities, are emotionally disturbed, are a member of a minority or sibling group that needs to be adopted as one.

Although the definition of "special needs" kids is constantly in flux, one agency points to these certain common denominators:

• these children are currently living in a foster home, group home, or institution;

• they cannot return to their biological families because of previous abandonment, neglect, abuse, or death of parents;

• they need and want a permanent family who will love and care for them;

• they have love, energy, and commitment to share with a family who can see beyond labels that have prevented them from having a "forever" family of their own.[1]

One adoptive parent explains that the phrase "hard-to-place" has society—not the children themselves—as its source. These kids are harder to place than others not because of *their* disabilities but because society has historically found it hard to accept them.

An adoptive mother of several hard-to-place kids puts it this way:

> I want to run out on the streets and tell everybody what it's all about—that handicapped children are not burdens, that it is *they,* not us, who do the suffering. It's *their* legs that don't work, *their* eyes that don't see and *their* hands that don't do what they are supposed to do.[2]

In very recent history we see a society in which there are somewhat less "hard-to-place" children. There are still, however, approximately 150,000 kids in institutions and foster care who are six years or older; near-ly half are black, many from broken homes, many with disabilities like cere-bral palsy.[3]

More special children are being adopted today in part due to better publicity on their behalf. A few years ago, KOCO-TV in Oklahoma City pio-neered a program called "Wednesday's Child," which profiles special needs kids waiting to be adopted. In its first two years the KOCO-TV program profiled seventy-seven children; of these, fifty-seven have been adopted. There are now approximately fifty shows similar to this across the country.

Adoption exchanges (see following profiles) have been in operation for a number of years. They have grown in number and effectiveness in recent years. Their work has been enhanced and the matching process expedited by increased use of computers.

In addition, adoption eligibility requirements are less strict with special needs kids. Most agencies do not use income, religion or education as crite-ria. Many are open to single applicants.

It is very expensive for society to keep these special children in inter-mediate care. As of 1978, $280 million was spent every year in New York State alone on foster care and the related administrative costs.[4] The finan-cial burdens involved in adopting some of these children have made pro-spective adoptive families apprehensive.

The financial load has been made somewhat lighter for these families by the arrival of subsidy programs in all states except Hawaii. The subsidy amounts vary widely from state to state usually according to the needs of the child and what the state already pays for foster care. The aid may cover medical care, legal counsel, tutoring, etc.

The recent federal tax law allows parents who adopt hard-to-place kids to take deductions of up to $1,500 for their expenses, including agency and attorney fees.[5]

> Regardless of subsidies, the acceptance of many children with problems has surprised some workers in the field. As one said, "We didn't realize that people could stretch enough to adopt any child, a child with a problem, just as their own child might have."[6]

A young mother whose family includes both adopted and biological children recalled to me several conversations she had while pregnant with one of her children. "As friends, family and even strangers on the bus came to notice my expanding girth they would ask if I wanted a boy or a girl. When I replied that it didn't make any difference, *they* always added 'as long as it's healthy.' I always thought, 'What difference does that make? It doesn't have to be healthy; it may not be healthy. The child will still be my responsibility and my joy.' Regardless of the 'troubles' any of my kids have, they're my kids."

Within the group of children with special needs is a group social workers call "high risk." Another descriptive phrase for these children could be children in danger. A priest who works with placing and follow-up of high risk kids says: "Once a youngster gets caught in the child-welfare or juvenile justice system he or she is often in greater peril than in the abusive home."[7]

Which children are considered "high risk"? Child welfare professionals include the following in this group: white kids age thirteen and older, black kids age seven and older, sibling groups, and physically disabled kids.

Although one out of seven of the high risk children may end up with the adoptive parents giving the child back, an estimated eighty-five percent do remain with their first adoptive family. And nearly every child who is given back by his first adoptive family is later successfully adopted by a new family.[8] (In other words as one commentator puts it, "Adopting a so-called high-risk child is statistically safer than *marrying* the person of your choice."[9])

39

It is very helpful if the adoptive parents have relatively little stress in other areas of their lives. They need firm access to emotional support from a caring and enlightened social worker, other adoptive parents, family and friends—in other words, a good support group.

> Most parents who succeed are ordinary people with their share of flaky traits but with extraordinary openness in one area or another. Some people are very good parents, but they don't have that openness, that capacity to accept deviance. I don't mean approve of it, but accept it, live with it, and still feel connected with the child.[10]

Pearl Buck once said, "There are parents for every child born in the United States of America." This prophecy is both an already and a not yet. If you are trying to decide whether you might be waiting parents for a special needs child, several professionals can offer food for your reflections.

Patricia Kravik has edited *Adopting Children With Special Needs,* which includes the following from Joan McNamara about possible readiness or unreadiness to consider adopting a special child:

Under possible readiness—

1) You like children and enjoy the challenge of raising a family. If you are not a parent already, you may have had other kinds of exposure to children through volunteer work, teaching, or your own extended family, that have given you insight into the daily realities of being a parent.

2) You are a flexible person. You usually deal with frustration with patience and are open to changes in your expectations and life style.

3) You are able to view people for what they *can* accomplish, not what they cannot, and value them according to their own potentials.

40

4) You have had contact with people who have handicapping conditions.

Under possible unreadiness—

1) You see adoption of a child with special needs as a charitable gesture, because you feel sorry for or pity a child, or feel a duty toward him.

2) You think such adoption is exciting, romantic, or a good way to make a public or personal statement.

3) You feel that you couldn't raise an "ordinary" or "normal" child.

4) A child with special needs is a second choice for you; the waiting time for children you would prefer is too long or there aren't any of the kind you really want.

5) You place a high value on achievement and success, and have set kinds of goals for your children's futures.

6) You view yourself as a person who does not react well to change and stress.

7) Your chosen life style is set and the adoption of a child with special needs would disrupt the activities that are important to you.[11]

In *Adopting the Older Child,* author Claudia L. Jewett offers the following as an exercise in your decision-making:

1) Describe the type of child toward whom you have the most positive feeling. What does this child look like? How does this child respond? Is its response affectionate, self-reliant, inquisi-

41

tive, trusting, bright, independent, dependent, grateful? What kinds of activities can you visualize yourself engaging in with this child? Is there a particular age you enjoy most? Why?

2) Describe the type of child toward whom you have the least positive feeling. What does this child look like? How does this child respond? What kinds of problems can you envision with this child? Is there a particular age you enjoy least? Why?

3) How do you express affection?

4) What rules do you have in your house for children?

5) What kinds of children intimidate you?

6) What kinds of behavior do you feel unable or unwilling to accept—defiance, destructiveness, aggression, withdrawal, sullenness, immaturity? How do you define each of these behaviors? How is your tolerance limited?

7) What kinds of handicaps could you accept?

8) What do you feel might make your placement succeed? Fail?

9) Could you turn down a child you felt uneasy about?[12]

And, finally, Grace Sandness, an adoptive parent of special needs children, gives an exquisite description of the hardy and deep love involved in this parenting:

This business of love is inexorably bound to commitment—certainly a more deliberate, more conscious commitment than for birthparents, who usually slip into its confines more gradually and easily. For them, usually, love comes first; commitment naturally follows. For us, the opposite is true and the love is often slow in coming. Does this mean our love is less valid, less sincere? No . . . only more complex.[13]

Profiles follow of several agencies and exchanges which serve special needs children along with a list of additional organizations and resources in this area.

SPECIAL NEEDS ADOPTION: *Profiles*

AID TO ADOPTION OF SPECIAL KIDS (AASK)
3530 Grand Avenue
Oakland, California 94610
415-451-1748

What: Founded by Dorothy and Robert DeBolt ("Who are the De-
     Bolts? And Where Did They Get 19 Kids?") in 1973, AASK
     serves as an intermediary on a national level between adoptive
     parents and licensed adoption agencies. Acting as an adoption
     exchange, AASK sees that special kids find permanent adoptive
     homes where they can get love and care.

Serves: Homeless special needs children
     AASK promotes and facilitates legal adoption of hard-to-place
     children. AASK has been responsible for approximately 2,000
     children finding adoptive homes with families who give them the
     care they need.

How: A three-part program:

     1) AASK has established a nationwide *Exchange Program* to
       match special needs children with adoptive families.

2) AASK has a licensed adoption agency in Oakland, California which serves families within a $1^1/_2$ hour drive from the office.

3) AASK's *Volunteer Program* is a nationwide network of men and women who have created AASK chapters throughout the U.S. Through these chapters AASK is able to gain local support for legislation involving handicapped kids and adoption, as well as promote AASK's services with local agencies with which AASK works.

What You
Can Do:

1) *Adopt*

After it has been established that a family is suitable for adopting a child, AASK determines what kind of child or children the family wants. From extensive files, AASK tries to single out the most suitable child for the family. After this match is determined and agreed to, AASK sets about to find the appropriate adoption agency or social worker in the family's state to work with the appropriate agency or social worker in the child's state. This adoption exchange function cuts down greatly on the waiting time for adoptive families all over the country.

2) *Contribute*—AASK relies entirely on voluntary tax-deductible contributions from the general public to fund its programs and operations.

═══════════════

THE CAP BOOK, INC.
700 Exchange Street
Rochester, New York 14608
716-232-5110

What: THE CAP BOOK, Inc. is a clearinghouse, not an adoption agency, with the goal of bringing together children waiting for adop-

45

tion and adults wishing to adopt them. It is a national photo listing service which registers children from any place in North America who need extra help and exposure to find adoptive families.

Serves: Homeless special needs children
Every year more than 100,000 "hard-to-place" children wait to be adopted. These are not healthy newborn infants but older, physically handicapped or retarded or emotionally disturbed children living in temporary foster homes or institutions. There is no fee to register children in THE CAP BOOK.

How:

1) It transforms information and photos received from adoption agencies across the country into printed pages, giving positive yet realistic descriptions of each child registered. These pages make up THE CAP BOOK itself.

2) It circulates new pages by mail biweekly to each of its more than 400 subscribers throughout the country.

3) It receives inquiries from both adoption agencies and adoptive parents. These inquiries are referred to the agencies responsible for adoption placements.

4) It dispenses general information to potential families on how to prepare themselves for the adoption process and how to find adoption agencies in their own areas.

5) It provides a newspaper column, "A Child Is Waiting," which appears regularly in many newspapers throughout the country. Each week the organization also selects descriptions of children with especially complicated problems and submits them for publication in the *National Enquirer* which has a circulation of over four million.

6) THE CAP BOOK staff is also available as consultants on how to operate and use a photo listing service as well as on how to do additional publicity.

What You Can Do:

1) *Subscribe to THE CAP BOOK* itself. A $50 per year investment gives you THE CAP BOOK filled with the 450 currently listed children and the biographical material on new children waiting for adoption.

2) *Make a contribution* to THE CAP BOOK, Inc. Such a gift is fully tax deductible and will be used to expand the work of this unique organization.

3) *Spread the word about the thousands of children waiting for adoption.*

4) *Consider adopting* a waiting child.

_____

Family Builders Agencies

Children Unlimited, Inc.
Post Office Box 11463
Columbia, South Carolina 29211
803-799-8311

Family Builders by Adoption
P.O. Box 9202
North Berkeley Station
Berkeley, California 94709
415-531-5913

Family Builders by Adoption
5800 Cody Court
Arvada, Colorado 80004
303-425-1667

Lutheran Child and Family Services
7620 Madison Street
P.O. Box 186 (mailing address)
River Forest, Illinois 60305
312-771-7180

Medina Children's Service—TASC
123—16th Avenue, P.O. Box 22638
Seattle, Washington 98122
206-324-9470

New York Spaulding for Children*
22 West 27th Street, 10th Floor
New York, New York 10001
212-696-9560

*One of several adoption agencies in the U.S. named after Warren Spaulding, who gave his home to the first Spaulding agency set up in Michigan in 1968.

Peirce-Warwick Adoption Service
5229 Connecticut Avenue, N.W.
Washington, D.C. 20015
202-966-2531

Permanent Families for Children
Child Welfare League of
    America, Inc.
67 Irving Place
New York, New York 10003
212-254-7410

Project CAN, Family Service Centers
2960 Roosevelt Boulevard
Clearwater, Florida 33520
813-531-0481

Project IMPACT
25 West Street
Boston, Massachusetts 02111
617-451-1472

Spaulding for Children
3660 Waltrous Road
Chelsea, Michigan 48118
313-475-8693

Spaulding for Children
36 Prospect Street
Westfield, New Jersey 07090
201-233-2282

Spaulding for Children
(Beech Brook)
3737 Lander Road
Cleveland, Ohio 44124
216-464-4445

Spaulding Midwest
1855 N. Hillside
Wichita, Kansas 67214
316-686-9171

Spaulding Southwest
4219 Richmond Avenue, Suite 100
Houston, Texas 77027
713-850-9707

Women's Christian Alliance
1610-1616 North Broad Street
Philadelphia, Pennsylvania 19121
215-236-9911

What: A network of sixteen adoption agencies begun in 1975, Family Builders Agencies work in close collaboration with The North American Center on Adoption, 67 Irving Place in New York City. The network's member agencies have secured adoptive homes for hundreds of children labeled "hard to place."

Serves: Homeless special needs children
Services include—

1) Preparing special children for adoption
2) Finding and preparing parents to adopt these special children
3) Providing help for the new families created

4) Helping other agencies with the adoptive placement of special children

How: 1) Charges no fees of adoptive parents; seeks reimbursement of full placement cost from referring agencies
2) Supplements existing adoption services
3) Collaborates with other agencies through accepting referrals on children needing families and sharing placement practice experiences
4) Provides other agencies with training and consultation in a variety of areas including recruitment techniques, parent/ child preparation, helping families after placement, purchase of service development

What You   1) *Adopt*
Can Do: Eligibility Policies—

- Applicants may be married couples, or men and women who are single, divorced or widowed.
- Applicants may be older.
- They may be childless or have other children.
- They may be renting or buying their own home.
- They may be employed or have another source of stable income, large or small. (Adoption subsidies can be arranged for some children.)

2) Contact the Family Builders Agency nearest you and offer your *support.*

NATIONAL ADOPTION INFORMATION EXCHANGE (NAIE)[14]
(formerly ARENA, NAIE's parent organization is the Child Welfare League of America)
67 Irving Place
New York, New York 10003
212-254-7410

49

What: NAIE is an adoption exchange which registers special needs, black and minority children available for adoption from local child placement agencies across the country.

Serves: Homeless special needs children
The majority of children available at NAIE are:

- School age boys, eight years and older with some degree of mental retardation

- Children of all ages with severe multiple physical, mental and/or emotional handicaps

- Down's Syndrome children nine years of age and older

- Black children whose agencies, for the most part, want black adoptive familes

- Black sibling groups, same as above

- Adolescents thirteen years of age and older

- Hispanic school age children with physical, mental and/or emotional handicaps and sibling groups

How: The Exchange provides information, public education, and publicity efforts for registered children, suggests or refers registered children for placement with adoptive families who have completed homestudies with local adoption agencies.

What You Can Do: 1) *Adopt*

- NAIE strongly suggests that you contact your local/state regional Adoption Resource Centers (list follows) about the special needs children available for adoption locally.
- To adopt a child a family must have a completed home study from a local agency. See Public and Licensed Private Adoption: Resources, for whom to contact in your state to obtain a list of licensed agencies. The Family Builders Agencies work closely with NAIE and can be found in

50

fourteen states and the District of Columbia as of this writing (see Family Builder Agencies profile in this section). One of these agencies could conduct your homestudy.

- If after your family has a completed homestudy you are interested in the children registered on the National Exchange, have your agency worker register you with the Exchange by calling 212-254-7410 ext. 422 for information about registration. You can also write or call directly if you are interested in a particular child on the Exchange. (See #6, Special Needs Adoption: Resources, to obtain information on waiting children.)

2) *Become better informed* on child welfare issues—NAIE's parent organization, The Child Welfare League of America, has a catalogue of all their publications, including books, monographs, research reports, audiovisual materials, and newsletter and journal subscriptions. With titles on adoption, foster parenting, residential group child care, and children in placement—and much more—the catalogue lists the most current literature available on all aspects of the child welfare field. Write Publications, CWLA, 67 Irving Place, New York, New York 10003.

SPECIAL NEEDS ADOPTION: *Resources*

1) Regional Adoption Resource Centers:

Region I Maine, New Hampshire, Vermont, Massachusetts, Connecticut, Rhode Island

Adoption Resource Center
286 Summer Street
Boston, Massachusetts 02210
617-426-8573

Contact: Jane Quinton (liaison—Joe Cronin)

Region II New York, New Jersey, Puerto Rico, Virgin Islands

Adoption Resource Center
Columbia University School of Social Work
622 West 113th Street—Suite 2
New York, New York 10025
212-280-4257

Contact: Abdul Rahmann Muhammad (liaison—Brenda Smalls)

Region III Pennsylvania, West Virginia, Virginia, Maryland, Delaware, District of Columbia

Adoption Resource Center
Delaware Valley Adoption Council
1218 Chestnut Street—Suite 204
Philadelphia, Pennsylvania 19107
215-925-0200

Contact: Marlene Piasecki (liaison—Toni Oliver)

Region IV North Carolina, South Carolina, Tennessee, Kentucky, Mississippi, Alabama, Georgia, Florida

Adoption Resource Center
University of North Carolina School of Social Work
143 West Franklin Street—Suite 314
Chapel Hill, North Carolina 25714
919-966-2646

Contact: Ann Sullivan (liaison—John Wolff)

Region V Ohio, Indiana, Illinois, Michigan, Wisconsin, Minnesota

Adoption Resource Center
University of Michigan School of Social Work
1015 East Huron Street, Social Work Center Bldg.
Ann Arbor, Michigan 48109
313-763-6690

Contact: Mary Hart (liaison—Pamela Dilley)

Region VI Louisiana, Arkansas, Oklahoma, Texas, New Mexico

Adoption Resource Center
University of Texas at Austin School of Social Work
2609 University Avenue—Suite 314
Austin, Texas 78712
512-471-4067

Contact: Rosalie Anderson (liaison—Zena Oglesby)

Region VII   Kansas, Nebraska, Missouri, Iowa

Adoption Resource Center
University of Missouri School of Social Work
124 Clark Hall
Columbia, Missouri 65201
314-882-6091

Contact: Johnnie Penelton (liaison—Glenna Wooderson)

Region VIII North Dakota, South Dakota, Montana, Wyoming, Colorado,
Utah

Adoption Resource Center
2695 Alcott Street—Suite 133
Denver, Colorado 80211
303-433-6413

Contact: Eugene Meeks (liaison—Judee Filipp)

Region IX   California, Nevada, Arizona, Hawaii

Adoption Resource Center
County of Los Angeles Department of Adoptions
2117 West Temple Street
Los Angeles, California 90026
213-738-3588

Contact: Louise Fleenor (liaison—Audrey Kahane)

Region X   Washington, Idaho, Oregon, Alaska

Adoption Resource Center
157 Yesler Way—Suite 206
Seattle, Washington 98104
206-382-0430

Contact: Karen Wernicke (liaison—Katherine Donner)

2) Any of the licensed public or private adoption agencies in your state will assist you in pursuing the possible adoption of a special needs child.

3) To locate groups in your area involved with special needs children and adoption contact the North American Council on Adoptable Children (NACAC), 1346 Connecticut Avenue, N.W., Suite 229, Washington, D.C. 20036, 202-466-7570.

4) Welcome House, P.O. Box 836, Beulah Road and Route 202, Doyles-town, Pennsylvania 18901, works with other child welfare agencies and with regional and national adoption exchanges to match waiting special needs children with adoptive families in Pennsylvania, Delaware, Virgin-ia, New Jersey, Maryland, the District of Columbia, and parts of New York and Connecticut. Eligibility: people of all racial, cultural and reli-gious backgrounds, married couples and single men and women who love children and who have happy, stable homes, people over twenty-one, of all income levels, people who can understand the special needs of children who have lived unsettled lives or have been neglected or abused or have physical or emotional handicaps. Call 215-345-0430.

5) The Edna Gladney Home, 2300 Hemphill, Fort Worth, Texas 76110, has established a program called New Hope for the placement of spe-cial needs children. These children are under the conservatorship of the Texas Department of Human Resources and the Home is part of a team that does recruitment, home studies, placement and on-going su-pervision of parents who can offer their homes and hearts to children with physical, mental or behavior problems. 24 hour phone service: Texas toll free #1-800-772-2740, National toll free #1-800-433-2922.

6) Permanent Families for Children, Child Welfare League of America, Inc., 67 Irving Place, New York, New York 10003 offers free of charge "Waiting Children," a memorandum (ten issues annually) featuring photos and profiles of children registered with the National Adoption Information Exchange System plus relevant articles.

7) Carney, *No More Here and There,* University of North Carolina Press, 1976

8) Featherstone, *A Difference in the Family: Life with a Disabled Child,* Basic Books: New York, 1980

9) Jewett, *Adopting the Older Child,* The Harvard Common Press, 1978

10) Kadushin, *Adopting Older Children,* Columbia University Press, 1970

11) Kravik (ed.), *Adopting Children With Special Needs,* Colophon Press: Kensington, Maryland, 1976

12) McNamara and McNamara, *The Special Child Handbook,* Hawthorn, 1977

13) "The Placement of a Large Sibling Group: A Cooperative Approach" is a step-by-step description of how two caseworkers placed a sibling group of seven in a single adoptive home. Interviewer David Thomas provides an orderly account of how such placements can be accomplished. Write LSDS, Dept 76, Washington, D.C. 20401 and request by the title and this number: (OHDS) 81-30305.

14) Sandness, *Beginnings, True Experiences in Adoption,* 1980

INTERCOUNTRY ADOPTION: *Remarks*

Parents who have adopted children from other countries report (often extreme) culture shock in their children regardless of whether the child was adopted as an infant or at an older age. "Children coming from overseas have suffered at least two losses of mothering persons and have gone through intense upsets and shifts in personal relationships and cultural patterns."[1]

These families point to a pervasive myth which surrounds infant adoption in particular. "This myth has been fostered by the lack of information given to new adoptive parents regarding the impact of change on infants."[2] The cultural environment the infant knows if only for a few months sets him up for an abrupt change when he deplanes in the United States. Frequently emotional problems result for the infant and for his adoptive family. Adoptive parents involved in intercountry adoptions urge those others about to adopt internationally to adequately prepare themselves now and to seek professional help for themselves and their adopted children when necessary later on.

Since most intercountry adoptions are also interracial adoptions, the conventional wisdom is that the visible differences of a child from another country serve up the greatest challenge to the adoptive family. Two mothers of "international children" place the emphasis elsewhere:

> Although (the multiracial aspect) is the most visible feature of
> our families to the outside world, and one that serves as a re-

57

minder to our (children) of their different origins, it is the family dynamics that affect us on a day-to-day basis, and those seem to be largely unrelated to race.[3]

Opinion against intercountry adoption centers around a resentment of what is perceived as capitalist paternalism:

The morality of adoption itself has been called into question by many of the groups who are currently supplying the greatest numbers of adoptable children. American blacks (see Issues) and the governments of many poor countries have objected to the movement for transracial and international adoption, which they see as compounding the injustices already visited upon them by the capitalist metropolis. In a system of gross economic inequality, they say, is it right that the weaker groups should be systematically deprived first of their ability to make a living, and then of the children they are unable to support?

On the other hand, the adopters reply, must the welfare and the very lives of children be imperiled while universal solutions to poverty are sought?[4]

The agenda of the United Nations General Assembly for Fall, 1982, shows discussion of the "Draft Declaration on Social and Legal Principles Relating to the Protection and Welfare of Children, With Special Reference to Foster Placement and Adoption Nationally and Internationally." (See Appendix for full text.) After giving the appropriate attention to the first priority for a child—to be cared for by the biological parents—the declaration moves on to the international possibilities if biological parenting is "unavailable or inappropriate":

- 19. Governments should determine the adequacy of their national services for children, and recognize those children whose needs are not being met by existing services. For some of these children, intercountry adoption may be considered as a suitable means of providing them with a family.

- 20. When intercountry adoption is considered, policy and legislation should be established to protect the children concerned.

- 21. In each country, placement should be made through authorized agencies competent to deal with intercountry adoption services and providing the same safeguards and standards as are applied in national adoptions.

- 22. Proxy adoptions are not acceptable, in consideration of the child's legal and social safety.

- 23. No adoption plan should be considered before it has been established that the child is legally free for adoption and the pertinent documents necessary to complete the adoption are available. All necessary consents must be in a form which is legally valid in both countries. It must be definitely established that the child will be able to immigrate into the country of the prospective adopters and can subsequently obtain their nationality.

- 24. In intercountry adoption, legal validation of the adoption should be assured in the countries involved.

- 25. The child should at all times have a name, nationality and legal guardian.

The National Directory of Intercountry Adoption Services points to four major sectors which provide services to American families adopting intercountry: state public welfare agencies, U.S.-based international child-placing agencies, domestic child-placing agencies, and adoptive parent groups involved with international adoption.

Approximately three-fourths of the states themselves provide some kind of direct service to families adopting internationallly (see Public and Licensed Private Agency Adoption: Resources); the remaining one-fourth rely solely upon voluntary agencies within their state for provision of these services.

A fair number of U.S. agencies accept applications from families residing anywhere in the United States; some accept applications regionally or from a neighboring state only.

The cost of adopting a child from another country can go as high as $5,000 but the wait frequently is not longer than one and a half years. The amount of red tape you run into depends on the native country of the child involved.[5]

Among many excellent agencies listed in the National Directory of Intercountry Adoption Services (see Intercountry Resources) are Holt International Children's Services, a U.S.-based international agency founded in 1956 by Bertha and Harry Holt, and Welcome House, a domestic child-placing agency founded in 1949 by Pearl Buck. Profiles of these two agencies follow along with a list of additional agencies and resources in the area of intercountry adoption.

INTERCOUNTRY ADOPTION: *Profiles*

HOLT INTERNATIONAL CHILDREN'S SERVICES
P.O. Box 2880
Eugene, Oregon 97402
503-687-2202

What: The world's leading international adoption agency, Holt is now
           a leader also in developing programs for endangered children in
           third world countries.

Serves: Homeless children
           Services for the children, in order of importance—

           1) Keeps the child in his biological family
           2) Places him in an adoptive home in the same country
           3) Places him in an adoptive family of another country

How: Generally, Holt's role is to enable and process the adoption of
           homeless children by—

           1) Removing legal barriers to their adoption
           2) Recruiting adoptive parents
           3) Promoting understanding of the social, emotional, and cultur-
              al adjustments of the child and the family in an adoption

4) Applying legal and technical expertise to facilitate the adoption

5) Providing support services to the adoptive family and child after placement

6) Being available for consultation after legal adoption

What You Can Do:

1) *Adopt*

Eligibility Policies

- One parent must be a citizen of the United States.
- Applicants must be at least twenty-one years of age. There shall not be more than forty-five years' age difference between the older adoptive parent and the child to be adopted at the time of placement.
- Couples must be married at least two years before applying. The marriage must be stable, with a good relationship between husband and wife.
- There shall be at least one year between the arrival of each child in the family.
- Adoptive applicants must have reasonable child care plans.
- Single parent adoptions are possible but very limited. Single applicants should contact Holt requesting a single parent information sheet prior to submitting the application.
- Adoptive applicants must also meet individual foreign country requirements *even if foreign requirements are more restrictive than Holt requirements.*
- To be eligible to adopt a child, you must also satisfy the requirements of the United States Immigration and Naturalization Service, of the law of your state of residence, of Holt and of the local agency doing the adoption study.

2) Contribute to *Care Shares*—$10 per month brings special medical care such as braces, therapy and surgery to children under the care of Holt-funded programs.

3) Get involved with Holt *Parent Groups*—These groups are included in many services ranging from supporting waiting adoptive parents to advocating for children's rights everywhere.

4) Lend *Prayer* Support—Holt values and appreciates the support you can give through prayer.

5) Assist with *Special Projects*—Holt uses a variety of supplies, equipment, and personnel to carry on its services. Each time work is initiated in a new country, there are start-up costs, such as outfitting a child care center or foster homes. Groups or individuals can raise funds or donate goods to meet specific project needs from $50 to $5,000. Holt will send a list of projects for the consideration of you or your group.

6) Take part in the *Sponsorship* program—$25 per month provides milk, food, clothing, essential health care and temporary foster care until a permanent plan can be made for each child.

WELCOME HOUSE
P.O. Box 836, Beulah Road and Route 202
Doylestown, Pennsylvania 18901
215-345-0430

What: Welcome House is a private, non-profit adoption agency, based between New Britain and Doylestown, Pennsylvania, with branch offices in Philadelphia; Shippensburg, Pennsylvania; Hockessin, Delaware; Brooklyn, New York; and Richmond, Virginia. Since its founding, Welcome House has placed over 3,000 children from Asia and the United States. Although for years Welcome House has been known for its focus on intercountry adoptions of mostly Asian or Amer/Asian children, it is now broadening its

63

service to also meet the needs of U.S. children, particularly those with "Special Needs." (See Special Needs Adoption: Resources)

Serves: Homeless children
In Intercountry Adoptions, Welcome House provides adoption services for homeless children and sponsorships for adolescents from overseas, currently with the countries of Korea and the Philippines as well as Hong Kong. This serves the agency's first purpose: To place orphaned and abandoned children in permanent homes through national and international adoption. Its second purpose is to cooperate with indigenous agencies to develop child welfare services in harmony with their needs and consistent with Welcome House's purposes.

How: From Korea, Welcome House places school-age children (boys over five, girls over eight), including both Korean and bi-racial (usually Korean-black) children, sibling groups, children with physical handicaps, mental retardation, or emotional problems. Some younger children are being placed, but not frequently. Welcome House has a cooperating relationship with Holt Children's Services, Inc. in Seoul, Korea.

From the Philippines, Welcome House places school-age children (boys over five, girls over eight), sibling groups, children with physical handicaps, mental retardation, or emotional problems. Some younger children are being placed, but not frequently.

From Hong Kong, Welcome House places children ages two to sixteen, plus some children with developmental problems.

What You Can Do: 1) *Adopt*
Korea—Welcome House can only work with families in their direct service area (Delaware, Pennsylvania, Virginia) for the Korean Program. In addition

- There must be at least twenty-one years' difference between the youngest parent and the child.
- There shall be no more than forty years' difference between the oldest parent and the child.
- Adoptive parents must be over the age of twenty-five.
- They must be married at least three years.
- Korean agencies cannot accept single applicants.
- There are no religious restrictions.

Philippines—Welcome House can place Filipino children in all states except Washington. In addition, the Ministry of Social Services and Development of the Philippines prefers—

- two-parent families
- families with three or less children
- single applicants are not their priority although they can also be considered for older children of the same sex as the parent

Hong Kong—Welcome House can place children in Pennsylvania, Delaware, Virginia, New Jersey, Maryland, the District of Columbia, and parts of New York and Connecticut. In addition

- Single parents will not be considered.
- Preference will be given to parents married for at least a year.

2) Participate in *Partners in Caring*—$20 per month sponsorships are available through Welcome House for children in Korea who cannot leave the country.

3) *Contributions* and *Bequests* are welcome.

4) If you live in the Doylestown, Pennsylvania area, support the work of the *Thrift Shop* of Welcome House.

INTERCOUNTRY ADOPTION: *Resources*

1) *National Directory of Intercountry Adoption Services* Department of
   Health and Human Services—Children's Bureau
   P.O. Box 1182
   Washington, D.C. 20013
   (This directory contains names and addresses of American agencies
   specializing in foreign adoptions. Prepared by the American Public Welfare Association, the information includes child placing resources, social
   service agencies—federal and state—as well as foreign authorities, and
   lists U. S. service resources across the board for families wishing to
   adopt internationally.)

2) International Concern Committee for Children
   911 Cypress Drive
   Boulder, Colorado 80303
   (Publishes an annual *Report on Foreign Adoption* that lists organizations, individuals, and agencies, approximate costs and waiting periods,
   and types of children available. It also includes a reading list and sections pertaining to single-parent and direct adoptions. Nine *Report* updates are sent throughout the year as additional information becomes
   available. Cost of the *Report* and updates is $7.50. The ICCC also pub-
   lishes the *ICCC Listing Service,* which currently lists approximately sev-
   enty children from nine participating agencies and sixty families

searching for that special child. These are foreign-born children whose U.S. adoptions have been disrupted, and children who, because of age or physical condition, are desperately seeking adoption out of their birth-countries. Advanced medical techniques can improve or correct many conditions. Many need only cosmetic attention. This listing service including updates is also $7.50; with Family Register it is $12.50.)

3) Children's Services International
   P.O. Box 76676
   Atlanta, Georgia 30328
   (For infants, parents must travel. Singles welcome.)

4) Concerned Persons for Adoption
   656 Ridgewood Avenue
   Upper Montclair, New Jersey 07043
   (This is a parent group, not an agency. It has material covering South and Central American adoptions. Please send stamped, self-addressed envelope.)

5) Crossroads, Inc.
   4901 West 77th Street
   Minneapolis, Minnesota 55435

6) Dillon Family and Youth Services
   2525 East 21st Street
   Tulsa, Oklahoma 74114

7) Friends of Children of Viet Nam, Inc. (F.C.V.N.)
   600 Gilpin Street
   Denver, Colorado 80218
   (This agency no longer places Vietnamese children. They only place Korean children and can only accept formal applications from residents of the state of Colorado. They will accept preliminary applications from out-of-state and keep you on a waiting list in case the regulations of the Korean government again change. For Colorado residents: couples

must be twenty-five years of age to adopt and must have been married for at least three years. No single parents may adopt. The Korean Agencies will set individual policies.)

8) Joint Council on International Children's Services
600 Gilpin Street
Denver, Colorado 80218

9) Latin American Parent Association
National Headquarters
P.O. Box 72
Seaford, New York 11783
(This parent group provides information on adoption sources in Latin America. Please enclose stamped, self-addressed envelope.)

10) Love the Children
221 West Broad Street
Quakertown, Pennsylvania 18951

11) OURS, Inc.
20140 Pine Ridge Drive
Minneapolis, Minnesota 55303
612-753-4788

12) South American Missionary Evangelism (S.A.M.E.)
P.O. Box 2344
Bismarck, North Dakota 58502
(Christian homes preferred; children of all ages; singles okay.)

13) Adcock, "Intercountry Adoption—Where Do They Go from Here?" Bouldon-Haigh-Irwin Press, 1979

14) Caudill, *Somebody Go and Bang a Drum,* Dutton, 1974

15) Chinook, *Kim, A Gift From Vietnam,* World Publishing, 1969

16) Erichsen and Erichsen, *Gamines: How to Adopt from Latin America,* 1981

17) Holt, *Seed from the East,* 1956

18) Holt, *Outstretched Arms,* 1972

19) Wabill, *Chinese Eyes,* Herald Press, 1974 (also for children)

PUBLIC AND LICENSED PRIVATE AGENCY ADOPTION: *Remarks*

In addition to public agencies which are tax supported, there are licensed private adoption agencies which may be affiliated with a religious group or be non-sectarian. To be licensed by a state, the agency must meet certain minimum standards. Additional standards apply if an agency is also accredited by a professional organization such as the Council on Accreditation of Services to Families and Children.

Among agencies affiliated with religious groups are the Catholic Charities agencies. These agencies have been placing children for adoption for over two hundred years and it is a function carried on in most of the diocesan agencies across the country. These diocesan programs serve all members of the "adoption triangle" as well as the families of the biological parents—particularly in the case of the unwed adolescent pregnant girl. Problems of adolescent pregnancy are treated within a family context unless there are strong and compelling reasons to do otherwise.

The National Conference of Catholic Charities supports the following priniciples relative to adoption:

- that all adoptions should be conducted through licensed non-profit agencies;

- that the right of the young woman relinquishing her child to preserve her privacy permanently if she so chooses should be respected;

- that the right of adopting parents to make it a condition of the adoption that the identity of the child begins with the adoption and the earlier record remains closed should be respected;

- reopen adoptions: NCCC supports the position of the National Committee for Adoption and is encouraging members to work with adoption agency coalitions to have states adopt the model adoption registry act proposed by the committee ("An Act To Establish a Mutual Consent Voluntary Adoption Registry and To Provide for the Transmission of Nonidentifying Information on the Health History and the Genetic and Social History of Adoptees").

One well-known licensed private non-sectarian agency is The Edna Gladney Home in Fort Worth, Texas. The Gladney Home provides, in addition to comprehensive adoption services, a fine-tuned residential program for expectant out-of-wedlock mothers which is a model in the field. A profile of the Home follows.

Both religiously affiliated and non-sectarian licensed agencies will be included on the list you can obtain from your state welfare office. (See Public and Licensed Private Agency Adoption: Resources.)

PUBLIC AND LICENSED PRIVATE AGENCY ADOPTION: *Profiles*

THE EDNA GLADNEY HOME
2300 Hemphill
Fort Worth, Texas 76110
Texas toll free   # 1-800-772-2740   lines open 24 hours a
National toll free # 1-800-433-2922   day, 7 days a week

What: The Edna Gladney Home is a non-profit, non-sectarian licensed
           child placing agency which offers prompt supportive help to
           young women seeking guidance and practical assistance with an
           untimely pregnancy.

Serves: Young women and homeless children
           In 1981 there were 377 admissions into the programs and 364
           infants placed for adoption.

How: 1) Residential Services
              • The Home operates a residential treatment center program
                for adolescents who are pregnant out of wedlock and is

approved by the Joint Commission on Accreditation of Hospitals. This program serves approximately four hundred young women each year from all over the United States. The treatment program is directed by a clinical psychologist and a consultant psychiatrist and trained social-workers. Each young girl receives group therapy and individual counseling to help her deal with the traumatic crisis of the untimely pregnancy and set goals for her future.

- The apartment resident program is for young women who are from nineteen to twenty-five years of age and serves approximately two hundred women each year.
- The education program enables the junior and senior high school student to continue her education on campus in a fully accredited program. To protect the girl's confidentiality, her transcript is kept at a local high school. All residents are also encouraged to take part in courses of enrichment such as ceramics, arts and crafts, and gardening in the Home's greenhouse.
- The G.E.D. program enrolls many young girls who have dropped out of school.
- The Career Development Center offers vocational courses including PBX, keypunch, secretarial skills and nursing. Successful completion of any of these courses will qualify the graduates for employment.
- The Half-Way House program is an on-campus program to aid the young woman to continue her on the job training until she has the opportunity to get established.

2) Hospital Services—Duncan Memorial Hospital, a division of The Edna Gladney Home, serves the medical needs of the Home. The nineteen bed, twenty-six bassinet accredited facility is a completely equipped private hospital with a professional staff that provides comprehensive medical care for both mother and child.

73

3) Infant Adoption Services—The Home is a licensed child placing agency and a member of the National Committee for Adoption, which promotes adoption as a positive option. The social services provided are professional and give protection for all members of the triangle. A skilled professional staff considers each request for adoption services on an individual basis. The demand for infants has necessitated many qualified couples to endure a long wait. Post-adoptive services are provided by the social work staff and clinical psychologist through seminars, auxiliary visitation and individual counseling.

4) Non-Residential Services—The Community Services Division provides maternity services to non-residents. This program was developed with flexibility and an awareness of the needs of young women who cannot use the resident program as a resource. If placement services are needed, these are provided by the adoption department; also, referral services are available. Approximately two hundred young women use this program each year.

5) The New Hope Program—This program was established in 1979 for the adoptive placement of special needs children. The Home hopes to find loving homes for at least one hundred children each year.

6) Ancillary Services
   • Adult Adoptee Association Membership is open to all adopted men and women who have reached the age of eighteen years. The organization was formed to aid in the education of the public about adoption. Members have been active in public speaking, in direct services to expectant parents and in working to promote adoption as a positive way to build a family. The organization wishes to protect the rights to confidentiality of biological parents who make adoptive plans for their child.

- Adoptive Grandparents Association members have an adopted grandchild and support the services of the Home. Members have served as volunteers at the Home, in auxiliary projects and in sharing their love and resources to meet the needs of the home. They have participated in legislative matters both state and national.
- Auxiliaries with a total of over 1,600 volunteer members interpret agency services, raise funds to support those services, provide direct services to expectant parents and work toward positive legislation to protect members of the adoptive triangle.

What You Can Do:

1) *Spread the word* about the services of the Home.

2) *Contribute* to support the work of the Home.

3) *Volunteer your time* by joining an Auxiliary group. (Contact the Home for locations of Auxiliaries.)

4) *Adopt*—As stated, the demand for infants has necessitated many qualified couples to endure a long wait. The wait is not as long if you are interested in pursuing the possibility of adopting a special needs child.

PUBLIC AND LICENSED PRIVATE AGENCY ADOPTION: *Resources*

Where to write in your state for a list of public and licensed private adoption agencies—

ALABAMA: Bureau of Family and Children's Services
                    State Department of Pensions and Security
                    Administrative Building
                    64 North Union Street
                    Montgomery, Alabama 36130

ALASKA: Department of Health and Social Services
                    Alaska Office Building
                    350 Main Street
                    Juneau, Alaska 99811

ARIZONA: Department of Economic Security—Social Services
                    3435 W. Durango
                    Phoenix, Arizona 85009

ARKANSAS:
Individual and Family Services Section
Social Services Division
Department of Human Services
P.O. Box 1437
Little Rock, Arkansas 72203

CALIFORNIA:
State of California
Adoptions Branch
Department of Social Services
744 P Street
Sacramento, California 95814

COLORADO:
Department of Social Services
State Social Services Building
1575 Sherman Street
Denver, Colorado 80203

CONNECTICUT:
Department of Children and Youth Services
Adoption Resource Exhange
170 Sigourney Street
Hartford, Connecticut 06105

DELAWARE:
State of Delaware
Department of Health and Social Services
Division of Child Protective Services
New Castle, Delaware 19720

DISTRICT OF
COLUMBIA:
Family Services Administration
Department of Human Services
122 C Street, N.W.
Washington, D.C. 20001

FLORIDA:
Youth Services Program Office
Department of Health and Rehabilitative Services
1317 Winewood Boulevard
Tallahassee, Florida 32301

GEORGIA:
Department of Human Resources
Division of Family and Children Services—
State Placement
618 Ponce de Leon Avenue
Atlanta, Georgia 30308

HAWAII:
Family and Children's Services
Public Welfare Division
Department of Social Services and Housing
P.O. Box 339
Honolulu, Hawaii 96802

IDAHO:
Bureau of Social Services, Division of Welfare
Department of Health and Welfare
Towers Building
450 W. State Street
Boise, Idaho 83720

ILLINOIS:
Department of Children and Family Services
1 N. Old State Capitol Plaza
Springfield, Illinois 62706

INDIANA:
Division of Child Welfare—Social Services
Department of Public Welfare
141 S. Meridian Street, 6th Floor
Indianapolis, Indiana 46225

IOWA:
Bureau of Children's Services
Division of Community Programs
Department of Social Services
Hoover State Office Building
Des Moines, Iowa 50319

KANSAS:
Children and Youth Services
Department of Social and Rehabilitation Services

Smith-Wilson Building, Topeka State Hospital
2700 W. 6th Street
Topeka, Kansas 66606

KENTUCKY: Department of Human Resources
                   Bureau for Social Services
                   275 East Main Street
                   Frankfort, Kentucky 40621

LOUISIANA: Office of Human Development
                   Department of Health and Human Resources
                   1755 Florida Boulevard
                   Baton Rouge, Louisiana 70802

MAINE: Division of Child and Family Services
                   Bureau of Resource Development
                   Department of Human Services
                   State House, Station 11
                   Augusta, Maine 04333

MARYLAND: Adoption Program
                   Social Services Administration
                   300 W. Preston Street
                   Baltimore, Maryland 21201

MASSACHUSETTS: Office for Children
                   120 Boylston Street
                   Boston, Massachusetts 02116

MICHIGAN: Office of Children and Youth Services
                   Department of Social Services
                   Commerce Center
                   300 S. Capitol Avenue
                   Lansing, Michigan 48913

MINNESOTA: Division of Social Services
Social Services Bureau
Department of Public Welfare
Centennial Office Building
658 Cedar Street
St. Paul, Minnesota 55155

MISSISSIPPI: Adoption Unit
Department of Public Welfare
P.O. Box 352
Jackson, Mississippi 39205

MISSOURI: State of Missouri Family Services
P.O. Box 88
Jefferson City, Missouri 65103

MONTANA: Child and Youth Development Bureau
Community Services Division
Department of Social and Rehabilitation Services
P.O. Box 4210
Helena, Montana 59601

NEBRASKA: Center for Children and Youth
Department of Public Welfare
5701 Walker Street
Lincoln, Nebraska 68504

NEVADA: Nevada State Welfare Division
Department of Human Resources
251 Jeanell Drive
Carson City, Nevada 89710

NEW HAMPSHIRE: Division of Welfare
Department of Health and Welfare
Hazen Drive
Concord, New Hampshire 03301

NEW JERSEY: State of New Jersey
               Division of Youth and Family Services
               Department of Human Services
               1 South Montgomery Street
               Trenton, New Jersey 08625

NEW MEXICO: New Mexico Human Services
               Children and Youth
               104 PERA Building
               P.O. Box 2348
               Santa Fe, New Mexico 87503

NEW YORK: Bureau of Child Protective Services
               Division of Services
               Department of Social Services
               40 N. Pearl Street
               Albany, New York 12243

NORTH   Division of Social Services
CAROLINA: 325 N. Salisbury Street
               Raleigh, North Carolina 27611

NORTH DAKOTA: Social Services Board
               Russell Building, Highway 83 N.
               Bismarck, North Dakota 58505

OHIO: Bureau of Children Services
               Division of Social Services
               Department of Public Welfare
               30 E. Broad Street
               Columbus, Ohio 43215

OKLAHOMA: State of Oklahoma
               Department of Human Services
               P.O. Box 25352
               Oklahoma City, Oklahoma 73125

OREGON: Oregon Children's Services
           198 Commercial Street, S.E.
           Salem, Oregon 97302

PENNSYLVANIA: Office of Children, Youth, and Families
                 Department of Public Welfare
                 P.O. Box 2675
                 Harrisburg, Pennsylvania 17105

RHODE ISLAND: Department For Children and Their Families
                 610 Mount Pleasant Avenue
                 Providence, Rhode Island 02908

SOUTH   Division of Children and Family Services
CAROLINA: Department of Social Services
                 1535 Confederate Avenue, Ext.
                 Columbia, South Carolina 29202

SOUTH DAKOTA: Office of Children, Youth, and Family Services
                 Division of Human Development
                 Department of Social Services
                 Richard F. Kneip Building
                 Pierre, South Dakota 57501

TENNESSEE: Children's Services Commission
              Office of the Governor
              108 Parkway Towers
              404 James Robertson Parkway
              Nashville, Tennessee 37219

TEXAS: Texas Department of Human Resources
          P.O. Box 2960
          Austin, Texas 78769

UTAH: State of Utah Department of Social Service
         Children, Youth and Families

P.O. Box 2500
Salt Lake City, Utah 84110

VERMONT: Division of Social Services
Department of Social and Rehabilitation Services
Agency of Human Services
Osgood Building, Waterbury Office Complex
103 S. Main Street
Waterbury, Vermont 05676

VIRGINIA: Commonwealth of Virginia
Department of Welfare
Blair Building
8007 Discovery Drive
Richmond, Virginia 23288

WASHINGTON: Bureau of Children's Services
Department of Social and Health Services
Adoption Program OB 41-C
Office Building 2
Olympia, Washington 98504

WEST VIRGINIA: West Virginia Adoption Exchange
P.O. Box 2942
Charleston, West Virginia 25330

WISCONSIN: Bureau of Children, Youth, and Families
Division of Community Services
Department of Health and Social Services
570 Wilson Street State Office Building
Madison, Wisconsin 53702

WYOMING: Division of Public Assistance and Social Services
Department of Health and Social Services
Hathaway Building
2300 Capitol Avenue
Cheyenne, Wyoming 82002

GUAM: Department of Public Health and Social Services
Division of Social Services
P.O. Box 2816
Agana, Guam 96910

PUERTO RICO: Department of Social Services
G.P.O. Box 11398
San Juan, Puerto Rico 00910

NATIONAL AND LOCAL ADVOCATES/ SUPPORT GROUPS:
Remarks

    A large number of organizations advocate for homeless children and adoption and lend support to those who adopt. Profiled on the following pages are three: the New York Council on Adoptable Children (a local group), the National Committee for Adoption, and the North American Council on Adoptable Children. These organizations themselves are very valuable resources in the field.

NATIONAL AND LOCAL ADVOCATES/ SUPPORT GROUPS:
Profiles

THE NEW YORK COUNCIL ON ADOPTABLE CHILDREN, INC.
    (COAC)
875 Avenue of the Americas
New York, New York 10001
212-279-4525

What: COAC is a non-profit adoptive parent and citizen action group,
            an active member of New York State Citizen's Coalition for
            Children, which unites the efforts of twenty adoptive and foster
            parent groups statewide in efforts to reform child welfare in the
            state. COAC regards prospective adoptive parents as the most
            important resource for homeless children, and believes that an
            all-out effort of support and encouragement to prospective
            adopters is crucial.

Serves: Familes and homeless children
            COAC is a firm advocate for the right of a parentless child to a
            permanent adoptive home.

How: 1) Parent Services

- general information—COAC gladly answers any question pertaining to adoption.
- supporting—COAC has twenty volunteer counselors, all adoptive parents, who provide information and support to individual prospective parents by phone or in person.
- group meetings—COAC schedules regular meetings for special interests of adoptive parents. There are Prospective Adoptive Parent Meetings, Single Adoptive Parents, Older Child Adoption, Interracial Families, Black Adoptive Parents and Hispanic Family Groups.
- social activities—These include picnics, potluck suppers at churches and community centers and holiday parties so that the children, adopted and biological, can get together and have fun.

2) Public Education

- media—The best way to attract and inform people about adoption is by using community service time on radio and television. Both have been generous with spot announcements about COAC's services and some regularly give biographies of adoptable children.
- COAC Newsletter—A bi-monthly publication informs membership about what is happening at COAC and also about social and political issues affecting adoption. COAC publishes news, articles, letters received, book reviews—but, most important, pictures and biographies of adoptable children.
- Speakers—COAC members are available to talk to groups of persons interested in adoption and do so regularly. COAC staff and Board members are often called to testify at hearings and to meet with public officials.

3) Legislative—In cooperation with other groups COAC educates legislators and legislative staffs about the need for child welfare reform.

4) Data Collection and Reporting—COAC staff and volunteers carefully collect and record information from each family who enters their counseling program. The information is used for two purposes: (a) to coordinate and maintain New York City's only central referral file on prospective families, their backgrounds, and child preferences, and (b) to establish an effective monitoring mechanism, compiling information on agency performance and practices which can then be shared with legislators, interested citizens, and the agencies themselves.

What You Can Do:

1) *Become a member*—Anyone concerned with child welfare is welcome to join COAC. Most members are adoptive parents, usually of special needs kids, but it is not unusual for an adoption agency to join.

2) *Advocate for children* as an individual or as part of a group or organization.

NATIONAL COMMITTEE FOR ADOPTION
1346 Connecticut Avenue, N.W.
Washington, D.C. 20036
202-463-7559

What: NCFA is a national advocacy organization which works on behalf of infant adoption, building families, promoting permanent homes for children and encouraging adoption as an option for unmarried parents by improving and expanding services, providing information and technical assistance, and advocating good standards.

Serves: Families, homeless children, pregnant young single women and their families, adoption agencies and agencies providing pregnancy counseling and residential maternity services

How:
- supporting agency adoption to protect children and families
- supporting the right to confidentiality for those in the adoptive circle
- encouraging and serving non-profit agencies that provide adoption services and services to unmarried parents
- providing information about adoption, services to unmarried parents, and infertility
- working for sound standards of professional practice
- looking into the impact of current adoption practices on babies, unmarried parents and people who want to adopt
- developing and working with state committees for adoption
- educating the general public on the value of agency adoption and services to unmarried parents
- advocating in Washington, D.C. and in state capitols
- operating a National Adoption Hotline, M-F, 24 hrs./day: 202-463-7563

What You Can Do:

1) *Become a member*—write NCFA for application. For $25 or more you will receive a monthly newsletter, *National Adoption Reports.*

2) *Make a contribution*—NCFA is a charitable, tax exempt organization.

3) *Become better informed about adoption programs and law*—NCFA has published several items aimed at assisting States in their consideration of adoption law, including the "Model Act to Establish a Mutual Consent Adoption Registry," the "Model Act for the Adoption of Children with Special Needs," and the "Documentation Packet for Model Act for Children with Special Needs." NCFA's Bookstore has a list of adoption resources. Contact NCFA for more information.

=======================

NORTH AMERICAN COUNCIL ON ADOPTABLE CHILDREN (NACAC)
1346 Connecticut Avenue, N.W., Suite 229
Washington, D.C. 20036
202-466-7570

What: NACAC is a non-profit, broad-based coalition of volunteer adoptive parent and citizen advocacy groups, caring individuals, and agencies. Working together with such organizations as the Child Welfare League of America, National Council of Juvenile and Family Court Judges, and Children's Defense Fund, NACAC speaks for the needs of thousands of rootless children.

Serves: Homeless children and families

How: 1) Works to bring the needs of 500,000 waiting children to the attention of Congress and the federal government through:

- a national network of child advocates
- advocacy training workshops
- expert testimony
- monitoring of legislation and policy
- action bulletins to members
- linkage with national organizations serving children

2) Training and Education in Adoption Methods Program, consisting of five basic categories of programs that make up a full range of partnership services provided by adoption agencies and parent groups including

- Information and public education
- Recruitment of families
- Parent preparation and training
- Post placement support
- Child advocacy

3) Through services to members including:

- *Adoptalk,* a monthly newsletter devoted to issues in adoption, foster care and parenting
- Adoption Week, an annual event held during Thanksgiving week to focus attention on the needs of waiting children, especially those who have special needs (are school-age, mentally, physically or emotionally limited, of sibling groups needing to be adopted as one, or of minority heritage)
- NACAC Conferences, the only continent-wide bi-annual conference on adoption uniting the concerns and resources of experienced adoptive parents and child welfare professionals
- Information and Resources, a wealth of information on adoption, including recommended books, a directory of parent groups and other printed material

What You Can Do: 1) *Become a member*—for general information, subscriptions and membership (individuals—$15; citizen adoption groups—depending on the group size; agencies and other organizations—$50) write the national office in Washington, D.C.

2) *Become better informed about NACAC* and its programs. Write Laurie Flynn, Executive Director, at the national office in Washington, D.C.

IV.

Federal/Corporate/ State Activity: Laws and Policies

"Let the little children come to me; do not stop them; for it is to such as these that the Kingdom of God belongs."

—Mark 10:14

Federal Level

Two major pieces of recent federal legislation have supported efforts for adoption. In 1978 Congress passed the first federal legislation on adoption—P.L. 95-266, the Child Abuse Prevention and Treatment and Adoption Reform Act (the Adoption Opportunities Act) which was reauthorized in 1981 for two years. The act provided for the establishment of a National Resource Exchange which lists waiting children and waiting parents and also keeps track of children in foster care. The Act established the Adoption Resource Centers regionally (see Special Needs Adoption: Resources, for list), and also mandated issuance of model state adoption legislation by the Secretary of Health and Human Services. A result, the Model Act for the Adoption of Children with Special Needs, was published in Fall, 1981. This model legislation was prepared by the Model Adoption Legislation and Procedures Advisory Panel.

From the introduction to the act:

> The Model Act is suggested legislation for the States to enact. It is not Federal law or regulation, nor will States be required to enact it in order to receive Federal reimbursement for services. Each state remains free to select from among the many provisions of the Model Act those which it finds will improve its existing adoption services for children with special needs and their birth and adoptive parents. . . . Congress intended (the Model Act): To eliminate barriers to adoption and to provide home environments for waiting children with special needs who would benefit by adoption.

The Philosophy of the Model Act—

The Model Act is the first comprehensive adoption law for children with special needs developed under Federal sponsorship. It has been written at a time when national attention has been focused on the many children in institutional or foster care for whom adoption might offer a permanent family. To increase the likelihood that children with special needs who need adoption services are identified and then placed for adoption, the Model Act focuses on ameliorating or eliminating various obstacles to adoption which exist in present law and practice. The Model Act concentrates on those obstacles which an adoption law can reasonably be expected to reach: the barriers in the legal process and in the operation of public and voluntary adoption agencies. The Model Act also provides for a range of adoption services to these children. Counseling and other services are made available to birth parents, adoptive parents, and prospective adoptive parents at critical junctures throughout the adoption process. The purpose of these services is to provide all parties with the full information they need to make informed decisions, decisions which will have a lifelong effect both for themselves and for a child.

To obtain a copy of the Model Act, write the Administration for Children, Youth and Families, 400 6th Street, S.W., Washington, D.C. 20201.

In June, 1980, Congress passed The Adoption Assistance and Child Welfare Act of 1980, which catalogued many "firsts" for children:

1) federal aid for adoption of special needs children

2) states required to establish an adoption assistance program by October 1, 1982

3) federal assistance for foster care mandates provision of pre-placement preventive services to help kids remain with their families

4) federal assistance for foster care mandates increased services and procedures to achieve the goal of permanent planning for children

5) federal government offers financial incentives to states to redirect child welfare programs to a family orientation, rather than placement of children

6) states required to conduct an inventory of all children in foster care under their supervision for six months or more

7) states must develop a service program planned to help children return to their families or where appropriate be placed for adoption, or legal guardianship

8) federal funding provided to support the voluntary placement of a child without judicial determination (previously federal AFDC matching funds were not available for children placed in foster care without judicial determination)

9) federal payments authorized for placement of children in smaller public institutions (serving no more than twenty-five children)—advances possible use of group homes for adolescents who cannot remain at home or live with a foster family[1]

Although it appears that these "firsts" might *add* to administrative costs, the Congressional Budget Office has estimated that the incentives for adoption provided in the act would actually *reduce* administrative costs for foster care by four billion dollars over five years.[2]

In other legislative action at the federal level, the Internal Revenue Service Code was amended in 1981 to permit a tax deduction of up to $1,500 for adoption of a special needs child (child must be AFDC or SSI eligible). This particular legislative action again serves the very worthy goal of further eliminating barriers to the permanent adoption of special needs kids.

Ideally, at some future time the parents of adopted children—regardless of whether the child is special needs or not—will be able to take federal tax deductions for certain adoption expenses, just as biological parents take tax deductions for the medical expenses associated with birth.

Corporate Level

The number of companies offering adoption benefits to their employees would increase if the federal government ceased to regard the benefits as taxable income.

The Ideal:

- firms routinely offering adoption benefits as well as maternity leave for the adoptive parent
- insurance policies that cover expenses incurred in adopting

The Real:

- Approximately twenty firms nationwide that offer adoption benefits to their employees and virtually none that offer maternity leave for the adoptive parent

- insurance policies (some) that cover pregnancy of a dependent daughter

The companies which now provide adoption benefits include American Can Company, Hallmark Cards and Pitney-Bowes. It has proved to be a relatively inexpensive activity. In the first six years of the Pitney-Bowes program, $50,000 was spent for seventy-six adoptions.[3]

The amounts of the benefits are "roughly equivalent to those they give new mothers. Some companies pay a fixed allowance; others reimburse specific expenses, such as agency fees and court and legal fees incurred by the adopting couple. In a few cases, such additional expenses as the cost of a medical examination for the child and even pregnancy expenses for the (biological) mother are reimbursed . . . one company, which bases its adoption benefit on the latest three-month average of pregnancy costs in its area, is now up to $2,200 per adoption."[4]

It is the feeling of those in the employee-benefit field that more employers would offer the optional adoption benefits in flexible benefit programs if these benefits were not taxable. Attempts have been made in Congress to exempt employee adoption benefits but the Treasury Department is foursquare against it.

State Level Activity

All states except Hawaii have their own subsidy programs for adoption of special needs kids. The subsidy programs vary a great deal in what they will subsidize and to what extent. Some states pay relatively little and for varying lengths of time post-adoption. On the other hand there are states like California which offers maintenance subsidies for five years after adoption. For subsidy information about your specific state contact any public or licensed private adoption agency in your state.

As to state level statutes and regulations regarding the adoption process itself—who may adopt, residency requirements, etc.—see the following table for information about your own state. Adoption agency staff and your attorney can fill you in on the finer legal points applicable in your state regarding the adoption process.

TABLE OF INFORMATION

(*NOTE: States with asterisk did not respond to questionnaire; information for these states, therefore, is dated and of a secondary nature.)[5]

STATE	WHO MAY BE ADOPTED?	WHO MAY ADOPT?	PETITIONER MUST RESIDE IN STATE?
Alabama	• minors • adults in certain cases	• "any proper adult person" • adult = over nineteen	• No • Petition may be filed in county of legal residence of petitioner, or where child resides, or where agency is which holds custody.
*Alaska	• persons of any age	• any person	• No
Arizona	• minors	• any adult resident of the state, whether married, unmarried or legally separated • a husband and wife jointly • adult = over eighteen	• Yes • Adoption proceedings shall be brought in the court of the county where the petitioner resides.
Arkansas	• persons of any age	• a husband and wife together although one or both are minors	• No • Petition may be filed where petitioner resides,

State			
California	persons of any age	• an unmarried adult • a married individual w/o the other spouse joining as a petitioner under certain conditions	where child resides, or where agency is located.
*Colorado	persons of any age	• an adult ten years older than adoptee, except in adult adoptions	• Yes • Petition must be filed in county of residence of petitioner.
Connecticut	persons of any age	• any person • over twenty-one	• No
Delaware	persons of any age	• any person	• No • Petition may be filed where agency is located or where adoptive parent resides.
	persons of any age	• unmarried person • a husband and wife • divorced or legally separated person • over twenty-one	• Yes • Petition may be filed where petitioner resides or where agency is located.
*District of Columbia	persons of any age		

TABLE OF INFORMATION (*cont.*)

STATE	WHO MAY BE ADOPTED?	WHO MAY ADOPT?	PETITIONER MUST RESIDE IN STATE?
*Florida	• persons of any age	• an adult	• Yes
Georgia	• persons of any age	• persons at least twenty-five years of age or • married and living with husband or wife • petitioner(s) must be at least ten years older than the child	• Yes • Petition may be filed in the county of petitioner or if good cause is shown, where the child resides or where the agency is located.
Hawaii	• persons of any age	• any proper adult person	• No • Petition may be filed where petitioner resides, where child resides, or where agency is located.
Idaho	• persons of any age	• the person adopting a child must be at least fifteen years older than the person adopted	• Yes • Petition must be filed where petitioner resides.

State	Who may be adopted	Who may adopt	Residency requirements for petition
Illinois	persons of any age	"a reputable person of legal age and of either sex" who "is under no legal disability . . ." / "a minor, by leave of court upon good cause shown"	Yes / Petition may be filed where petitioner resides, where child resides, or where agency is located.
*Indiana	persons of any age	persons over twenty-one	Yes
Iowa	persons of any age	an unmarried adult / husband and wife together / husband and wife separately under certain conditions	No / Petition may be filed where petitioner resides, where child resides, or where agency is located.
Kansas	persons of any age	any person or persons / twenty-one years of age or older	No / Petition may be filed where petitioner resides, where child resides, or where agency is located.
Kentucky	persons of any age	any state resident / eighteen years of age or older	Yes / Petition must be filed where petitioner resides.
*Louisiana	persons of any age	any person	No

TABLE OF INFORMATION (cont.)

STATE	WHO MAY BE ADOPTED?	WHO MAY ADOPT?	PETITIONER MUST RESIDE IN STATE?
Maine	• persons of any age	• any unmarried person • any husband and wife jointly	• No • Petition may be filed where petitioner resides, where child resides, or where agency is located.
Maryland	• persons of any age	• any person • over eighteen years of age	• No • Petition may be filed where petitioner resides, where child resides, or where agency is located.
Massachusetts	• persons of any age	• a person of full age • a minor under certain conditions	• No • Petition must be filed where child resides if petitioner is not a resident. If a resident, petition may be filed in court of the county where petitioner resides.

State	Who May Be Adopted	Who May Adopt	Residence/Jurisdiction
Michigan	• persons of any age	• any person • with husband or wife if married • eighteen years of age or older	• No • Petition may be filed where petitioner resides or where child resides.
Minnesota	• persons of any age	• any person and spouse, if there be one	• Yes, unless court waives residence • Petition must be filed where petitioner resides.
Mississippi	• persons of any age	• an unmarried adult • a married person whose spouse joins in the petition	• Yes • Petition may be filed where petitioner resides, where child resides, or where agency is located.
Missouri	• persons of any age	• no definition	• No • Petition may be filed where petitioner resides or where child resides.
Montana	• persons of any age	• a husband and wife • an unmarried person • married but legally separated person • unmarried mother or father	• Yes • Petition must be filed where petitioner resides.

TABLE OF INFORMATION (*cont.*)

STATE	WHO MAY BE ADOPTED?	WHO MAY ADOPT?	PETITIONER MUST RESIDE IN STATE?
Nebraska	• minors	• any adult person • adult = nineteen or over	• No • Petition must be filed where petitioner resides.
Nevada	• persons of any age	• any adult person • any two persons married to each other	• Yes, for a period of 6 months • Petition may be filed where petitioner resides, where child resides, or where agency is located.
New Hampshire	• persons of any age	• anyone	• No • Petition may be filed where petitioner resides, where child resides, or where agency is located.
New Jersey	• minors	• any adult person • adult = eighteen years of age or over • must be at least ten years older than the child to be adopted	• No • Petition may be filed where petitioner resides or where agency is located.

State			
New Mexico	• minors to age 18	• any person fit to be a parent	• No • Petition may be filed where petitioner resides, where child resides, or where agency is located.
*New York	• persons of any age	• adults	• Yes
North Carolina	• persons of any age	• any person over eighteen • if married, the spouse shall join in the petition if competent to do so	• Yes • Petition may be filed where petitioner resides, where child resides, or where agency is located.
North Dakota	• persons of any age	• a husband and wife together although one or both are minors • an unmarried adult • the unmarried father or mother of the individual to be adopted • a married individual w/o the other spouse joining as a petitioner under certain conditions	• Yes • Petition may be filed where petitioner resides or where agency is located.

TABLE OF INFORMATION (*cont.*)

STATE	WHO MAY BE ADOPTED?	WHO MAY ADOPT?	PETITIONER MUST RESIDE IN STATE?
Ohio	• minors • adults under certain conditions	• married couple if one is adult • single adult • minor parent of child to be adopted	• No • Petition may be filed where petitioner resides, where child resides, or where agency is located.
Oklahoma	• persons of any age	• unmarried person who is at least twenty-one • married person who is at least twenty-one • a husband and wife jointly, or either if the other is parent of the child	• Yes • Petition must be filed where petitioner resides.
Oregon	• persons of any age	• any person • if married, spouse must join in the petition	• No, but child or petitioner must be resident of Oregon • Petition may be filed where petitioner resides, where child resides, or where agency is located.

State				
Pennsylvania	• persons of any age	• "any individual may become an adopting parent"	• No	• Petition may be filed where petitioner resides, where child resides, or where agency is located.
*Rhode Island	• persons of any age but younger than adopter	• any person	• Yes	
South Carolina	• persons of any age	• any person of legal age • legal age = eighteen	• No	• Petition may be filed where child resides or where agency is located.
South Dakota	• persons of any age	• any qualified person • at least ten years older than adopted child	• Yes	• Petition may be filed where petitioner resides, where child resides, or where agency is located.
Tennessee	• persons of any age	• any qualified person over eighteen years of age	• Yes	• Petition may be filed where petitioner resides, where child resides, or where agency is located.

TABLE OF INFORMATION (*cont.*)

STATE	WHO MAY BE ADOPTED?	WHO MAY ADOPT?	PETITIONER MUST RESIDE IN STATE?
Texas	• persons of any age	• any adult	• No • Petition may be filed where petitioner resides, where child resides, or where agency is located, if court is willing to transfer jurisdiction.
Utah	• persons of any age	• any adult person • a married person cannot adopt without the consent of the spouse unless legally separated • must be at least ten years older than the child adopted	• No • Petition must be filed where petitioner resides.
Vermont	• persons of any age	• adult of sound mind	• No

State	Who may be adopted	Who may adopt	Jurisdiction / Where petition is filed
Virginia	• minors • adults under certain conditions	• any living person residing in state or having custody of child placed by a Virginia agency	• No • Petition may be filed where petitioner resides or where agency is located.
Washington	• persons of any age		• Yes • Petition must be filed where petitioner resides.
West Virginia	• persons of any age	• any person • must be at least fifteen years older than the child to be adopted—can be waived at the judge's discretion	• Yes • Petition must be filed where petitioner resides.
Wisconsin	• persons of any age	• a husband and wife jointly or either if the other spouse is parent of the child • an unmarried adult	• Yes • Petition must be filed where child "is."

TABLE OF INFORMATION (cont.)

STATE	WHO MAY BE ADOPTED?	WHO MAY ADOPT?	PETITIONER MUST RESIDE IN STATE?
Wyoming	• persons of any age	• any resident of Wyoming may be single • twenty-one or over	• Yes • Petition must be filed where petitioner resides.
Guam	• minors	• the husband and wife jointly, or either if the other spouse is a parent of the child • an unmarried adult • a married adult who is legally separated • must be ten years older than the child	• Yes
Puerto Rico	• persons of any age	• any person in full exercise of his or her civil rights • over twenty-one years of age • at least sixteen years older than the adoptee except under certain conditions	• Yes • Petition must be filed where child resides.

Appendix

UNITED NATIONS DRAFT DECLARATION

Draft Declaration on Social and Legal Principles Relating to the Protection and Welfare of Children, with Special Reference to Foster Placement and Adoption Nationally and Internationally (annexed to U.N. General Assembly resolution 36/167)

A. *General Family and Child Welfare*

1. It is in the best interest of every nation to give a high priority to family and child welfare as it plans for the use and further development of national resources.

2. It is recognized that the best child welfare is good family welfare.

3. It is affirmed that the first priority for a child is to be cared for by the biological parents. Other family members should be the first alternative if the biological parents cannot provide care for the child.

4. When biological family care is unavailable or inappropriate, substitute family care should be considered.

5. It must be recognized that there are parents who cannot bring up their own children and that the children's rights to security, affection and continuing care should be of greatest importance.

6. Providers of service should have professional social work training in family and child welfare.

B. *Foster Placement*

7. Every child has a right to a family. Children who cannot remain in their biological family should be placed in foster family or adoption in preference to institutions, unless the child's particular needs can best be met in a specialized facility.

8. Children for whom institutional care was formerly regarded as the only option should be placed with families, both foster and adoptive.

9. Provision should be made for regulation of placement of children outside of their biological family.

10. Foster family care should be a planned, temporary service as a bridge to permanency for a child, which includes but is not limited to restoration to the biological family or adoption.

11. Planning for the child in foster family care must involve the biological family, foster family and child, if appropriate, under the auspices of a competent authorized agency.

C. *Adoption*

12. The primary purpose of adoption is to provide a permanent family for a child who cannot be cared for by his/her biological family.

13. Adoption procedures should be flexible enough to meet the child's needs in various situations.

14. In considering possible adoption placements, those responsible for the child should select the most appropriate environment for the particular child concerned.

15. Sufficient time and adequate counselling should be given to the biological parents to enable them to reach a decision on their child's future, recognizing that it is in the child's best interest to reach this decision as early as possible.

16. Legislation and services should ensure that the child becomes an integral part of the adoptive family.

17. The need of adult adoptees to know about their background should be recognized.

18. There should be recognition, in the law, of traditional adoption within the family, to ensure the protection of the children and to assist the family by counselling.

19. Governments should determine the adequacy of their national services for children, and recognize those children whose needs are not being met by existing services. For some of these children, intercountry adoption may be considered as a suitable means of providing them with a family.

20. When intercountry adoption is considered, policy and legislation should be established to protect the children concerned.

21. In each country, placements should be made through authorized agencies competent to deal with intercountry adoption services and providing the same safeguards and standards as are applied in national adoptions.

22. Proxy adoptions are not acceptable, in consideration of the child's legal and social safety.

23. No adoption plan should be considered before it has been established that the child is legally free for adoption and the pertinent documents necessary to complete the adoption are available. All necessary consents must be in a form which is legally valid in both countries. It must be definitely established that the child will be able to immigrate into the country of the prospective adopters and can subsequently obtain their nationality.

24. In intercountry adoption, legal validation of the adoption should be assured in the countries involved.

25. The child should at all times have a name, nationality and legal guardian.

BIBLIOGRAPHICAL MATERIAL

These books include plenty of personal narrative or references to case studies:

Blank, J. P. *19 Steps Up the Mountain: The Story of the DeBolt Family.* Adoptalk, 6 Madison Avenue, Ossining, New York 10562.

Chinook. *Kim, A Gift from Vietnam.* World Publishing: New York, 1969.

Cohen, J. S. *Adoption Breakdown with Older Children.* Available through the Faculty of Social Work, University of Toronto, 246 Bloor Street West, Toronto, Ontario, M5S 1A1 for $4.

Fisher, F. *The Search for Anna Fisher.* Arthur Fields Books: New York, 1973.

Jewett, C. *Adopting the Older Child.* The Harvard Common Press: Cambridge, 1978.

Klibanoff, S. and E. *Let's Talk About Adoption.* Little Brown and Co.: Boston and Toronto, 1973.

Lifton, B. J. *Twice Born: Memoirs of an Adopted Daughter.* Penguin Books: New York, 1977.

Lifton, B. J. *Lost and Found: The Adoption Experience.* The Dial Press: New York, 1976.

Margolies and Gruber. *They Came to Stay.* Coward McCann and Geoghegan: New York, 1976.

Pedersen, M. *At Sixes and Sevens.* World Publishing Co.: New York, 1969.

Sandness, G. *Beginnings, True Experiences in Adoption.* 1980.

Sorosky, Baran, Pannor. *The Adoption Triangle: The Effects of the Sealed Record on Adoptees, Birth Parents, and Adoptive Parents.* Anchor Press: Garden City, 1978.

Triseliotis. *In Search of Origins: The Experiences of Adopted People.* Routledge and Kegan Paul: London and Boston, 1973.

Other References:

Adoption Services in the States. U.S. Dept. of Health and Human Services, Administration for Children, Youth and Families, Children's Bureau, Washington, D.C. 20201, DHHS Pub. # (OHDS) 80-30288.

Bettelheim, B. *Love Is Not Enough.* Macmillan: New York, 1950.

Children Today. Bi-monthly journal of the DHHS Children's Bureau.

Dougherty, S. A. "Single Adoptive Mothers and Their Children." *Social Work,* July, 1978.

Feigelman, W. and Silverman, A. R. "Single Parent Adoption." *Social Casework,* July, 1977.

Goldstein, J., Freud, A., Solnit, A. J. *Beyond the Best Interests of the Child.* Free Press Paperback: New York, 1973.

Handbook for Prospective Single Parents. Prepared and distributed for the Single Parents Committee of Metropolitan Washington, 3824 Legation Street, N.W., Washington, D.C. 20015 ($1.75).

McNamara, J. *The Adoption Adviser.* Hawthorn Books: New York, 1975.

McNamara, J. and McNamara, B. *The Special Child Handbook.* Hawthorn Books: New York, 1977.

Raymond, L., revised by C. T. Dywasuk. *Adoption and After.* Harper and Row: New York, 1974.

Redinger, R. O. *Adoption: A Parent's Answers to Important Questions.* Grosset and Dunlop: New York, 1979.

Van Why, E. W. (annotated and compiled by). *Adoption Bibliography and Multi-Ethnic Sourcebook.* Open Door Society of Connecticut, Box 19, West Hartland, CT 06091 ($7.50).

Wishard, L. and Wishard, W. R. *Adoption: The Grafted Tree.* Cragmont, 1979.

ADDRESS LIST

Adoptee's Liberty Movement Association (ALMA)
P.O. Box 154
Washington Bridge Station
New York, New York 10033
212-581-1568

Aid to Adoption of Special Kids (AASK)
3530 Grand Avenue
Oakland, California 94610
415-451-1748

Catholic Social Services
P.O. Box 38
Green Bay, Wisconsin 54305

Children's Defense Fund
1520 New Hampshire Avenue, N.W.
Washington, D.C. 20036
202-483-1470

Children's Services International
P.O. Box 76676
Atlanta, Georgia 30328

Committee for Single Adoptive Parents
P.O. Box 4074
Washington, D.C. 20015

Concerned Persons for Adoption
656 Ridgewood Avenue
Upper Montclair, New Jersey 07043

Council of Adoptive Parents (The CAP BOOK)
700 Exchange Street
Rochester, New York 14608
716-232-5110

Crossroads, Inc.
4901 West 77th Street
Minneapolis, Minnesota 55435

Department of Health and Human Services
Administration for Children, Youth, and Families
Children's Bureau
Washington, D.C. 20201

Dillon Family and Youth Services
2525 East 21st Street
Tulsa, Oklahoma 74114

The Edna Gladney Home
2300 Hemphill
Fort Worth, Texas 76110
Texas toll free #1-800-772-2740
National toll free #1-800-433-2922

Family Builders Agencies (See Special Needs: Profiles)

Foster Parents Plan
1-800-621-5800

Friends of Children of Vietnam (F.C.V.N.)
also Joint Council on International Children's Services
600 Gilpin Street
Denver, Colorado 80218

Holt International Children's Services
P.O. Box 2880
Eugene, Oregon 97402
503-687-2202

International Concern Committee for Children
911 Cypress Drive
Boulder, Colorado 80303

International Social Service—American Branch
291 Broadway
New York, New York 10007

Latin American Parent Association
National Headquarters
P.O. Box 72
Seaford, New York 11783

Love the Children
221 West Broad Street
Quakertown, Pennsylvania 18951

National Adoption Information Exchange (NAIE)
Child Welfare League of America
67 Irving Place
New York, New York 10003

National Committee for Adoption
1346 Connecticut Avenue, N.W., Suite 326
Washington, D.C. 20036
202-463-7559

National Committee for Prevention of Child Abuse
332 South Michigan Avenue, Suite 1250
Chicago, Illinois 60604

National Council of Juvenile and Family Court Judges
P.O. Box 8978
University of Nevada
Reno, Nevada 89507
702-784-6012

National Urban League
500 East 62nd Street
New York, New York 10021

The New York Council on Adoptable Children (COAC)
875 Avenue of the Americas
New York, New York 10001
212-279-4525

North American Council on Adoptable Children (NACAC)
1346 Connecticut Avenue, N.W., Suite 229
Washington, D.C. 20036
202-466-7570

OURS, Inc.
20140 Pine Ridge Drive
Minneapolis, Minnesota 55303
612-753-4788

Regional Adoption Resource Centers (See Special Needs: Resources)

South American Missionary Evangelism (S.A.M.E.)
P.O. Box 2344
Bismarck, North Dakota 58502

The Adoption Book

State Child Welfare Addresses (See Public and Licensed Private Agency
    Adoption: Resources)

Welcome House
P.O. Box 836
Beulah Road and Route 202
Doylestown, Pennsylvania 18901
215-345-0430

NOTES

Adoption Overview

1. Mary Kathleen Benet, *The Politics of Adoption,* The Free Press, Macmillan Publishing Co., Inc.: New York, 1976, pp. 81-82.

2. Debra Cohen, "The American Experience Is Different," *Psychology Today,* November, 1977, p. 132.

3. M. K. Benet, *The Politics of Adoption,* p. 29.

4. Anne Langston, "Adoption and/or Foster Care," *Adoptalk,* February, 1982, p. 2. (Reprinted from the December, 1981 newsletter of the Oklahoma Council on Adoptable Children.)

5. John A. Calhoun, "The 1980 Child Welfare Act," *Children Today,* September/October, 1980, p. 3.

6. *Guidelines for Adoption Service,* abstracted from the Child Welfare League of America Standards for Adoption Service, Sally P. Ford, Editorial Consultant, Child Welfare League of America, Inc., 1971.

7. M. K. Benet, *The Politics of Adoption,* p. 11.

8. Morton L. Leavy, *Law of Adoption,* Oceana Publications, Inc.: Dobbs Ferry, New York, 1968, p. 1.

9. Maxine Phillips, "Adopting a Child," Public Affairs Pamphlet #585, Public Affairs Pamphlets, 381 Park Avenue South, New York, New York 10016, p. 4.

10. Jane Adonizio, "Man Uses Ads To Find Babies a Home," *The Times Leader,* Wilkes-Barre, Pennsylvania, February 17, 1982, p. 3A.

11. "If You Want To Adopt a Child," *U.S. News and World Report,* June 15, 1981, p. 54.

12. Robert A. Freitas, Jr., "Fetal Adoption: A Technological Solution to the Problem of Abortion Ethics," *The Humanist,* May/June, 1980, p. 22.

Baby Selling

1. Maxine Phillips, "Adopting a Child," Public Affairs Pamphlet #585, Public Affairs Pamphlets, 381 Park Avenue South, New York, New York 10016, p. 21.
2. Lynne McTaggart, "Babies for Sale," *Saturday Review,* November 10, 1979, p. 16.
3. "Brighter Days for 'Unadoptable' Children," *U.S. News and World Report,* October 16, 1978, p. 80.
4. L. McTaggart, "Babies for Sale," p. 15.

Independent Adoptions

1. Marie Weston Evans, "Independent Adoptions: In Whose Best Interests?" *The Oklahoma Bar Journal,* July 31, 1982, p. 1805.
2. W. Meezan, S. Katz, E. M. Russo, *Adoptions Without Agencies: A Study of Independent Adoptions,* The Child Welfare League of America, Inc.: New York, 1978, pp. 223-224.
3. *Ibid.,* p. 222.
4. Stephanie Azzarone, "New Options in Adoptions," *Money,* November, 1981, p. 98.
5. Meezan, Katz, Russo, *Adoptions Without Agencies,* p. 227.
6. M. W. Evans, "Independent Adoptions: In Whose Best Interests?" p. 1805.
7. *Guidelines for Adoption Service,* abstracted from the Child Welfare League of America Standards for Adoption Service, Sally P. Ford, Editorial Consultant, Child Welfare League of America, Inc., 1971, p. 1.
8. Meezan, Katz, Russo, *Adoptions Without Agencies,* p. 233.

Open Adoption

1. Maxine Phillips, "Adopting a Child," Public Affairs Pamphlet #585, Public Affairs Pamphlets, 381 Park Avenue South, New York, New York 10016, p. 24.
2. Informational letter, Catholic Social Services of Green Bay, Wisconsin, p. 2.
3. M. Phillips, "Adopting a Child," p. 25.

Sealed Records

1. Trudy R. Hayden, "The Rights of Parents and Children," *Current,* February, 1977, p. 29.
2. Margaret Mead, "In the Best Interests of the Child," *Redbook Magazine,* October, 1978, pp. 100, 188.
3. Mary Kathleen Benet, *The Politics of Adoption,* The Free Press, Macmillan Publishing Co., Inc.: New York, 1976, p. 191.
4. T. R. Hayden, "The Rights of Parents and Children," p. 30.
5. Bill McKay, "NCFA Submits Registry to State," *Ours,* a quarterly publication of The Edna Gladney Home, Spring, 1982.
6. *Ibid.*

Single Parent Adoption

1. Gini Kopecky, "What It's Like for Singles Who Adopt: Four Family Stories," *MS* Magazine, June, 1977, p. 45.
2. *Ibid.*
3. Kathryn Rose Gertz, "Single Parenthood," *Harpers Bazaar,* August, 1981, p. 185.
4. "Solo Parents and Adoptions," *Human Behavior,* January, 1978, p. 37, citing a study by W. Feigelman and A. R. Silverman.
5. Informational letter of the Committee for Single Adoptive Parents, p. 2.

Transracial and Mixed Race Adoption

1. Maxine Phillips, "Adopting a Child," Public Affairs Pamphlet #585, Public Affairs Pamphlets, 381 Park Avenue South, New York, New York 10016, p. 13.

2. *People,* December 22, 1980, p. 85.

Special Needs Adoption

1. Welcome House, Doylestown, Pennsylvania.

2. Phyllis Battelle, "Special Children, Special Joys," *Ladies Home Journal,* December, 1981, p. 66, quoting Rachel Rossow.

3. Mike Lipton, "The Children Nobody Wanted," *TV Guide,* August 1–7, 1981, p. 22.

4. Parker Rossman, "Adopting Teen-Agers: The Solution for Delinquency, An Interview With Father Paul Engel," *The Christian Century,* December 27, 1978, p. 1265.

5. Stephanie Azzarone, "New Options in Adoptions," *Money,* November, 1981, p. 94.

6. "Adopting a Child Today," *Changing Times,* April, 1977, p. 44.

7. P. Rossman, "Adopting Teen-Agers: The Solution for Delinquency, An Interview With Father Paul Engel," p. 1263.

8. Jane Marks, "Children of Crisis: True Tales of High Risk Adoptions," *New York,* February 5, 1979, p. 31.

9. *Ibid.,* p. 32.

10. *Ibid.,* quoting John Boyne, Executive Director of Spaulding for Children in Westfield, New Jersey.

11. Patricia Kravik (ed.) *Adopting Children With Special Needs,* Colophon Press: Kensington, Maryland, 1976.

12. Claudia L. Jewett, *Adopting the Older Child,* The Harvard Common Press: Cambridge, Massachusetts, 1978, p. 46.

13. Grace Sandness, "The Ways We Meet," *Adoptalk,* February, 1982, p. 4.

14. NAIE is one part of the National Adoption Information Exchange System (NAIES); the other two parts are Training and Technical Assistance provided through the regions, and Publications.

Intercountry Adoption

1. Holt brochure, "Adoption—A Family Affair," p. 3.
2. "Infant Adoption: Two Family Experiences with Intercountry Adoption," *Children Today,* November/December, 1980, p. 2.
3. *Ibid.,* p. 5.
4. Mary Kathleen Benet, *The Politics of Adoption,* The Free Press, Macmillan Publishing Co., Inc.: New York, 1976, p. 20.
5. Stephanie Azzarone, "New Options in Adoptions," *Money,* November, 1981, p. 96.

Federal/Corporate/State Activity: Laws and Policies

1. John A. Calhoun, "The 1980 Child Welfare Act," *Children Today,* September/October, 1980, pp. 2-3.
2. "Will Widows Be Next?" *The New Republic,* May 30, 1981, p. 8.
3. "Adoption Aid: Corporations Have Begun To Recognize That Parenthood by Any Means Can Be Costly," *Money,* December, 1980, p. 128.
4. "The New Corporate Goodies," *Dun's Review,* July, 1981, p. 49.
5. For states with asterisk, the information was taken from either one or both of the following sources: Morton L. Leavy, *Law of Adoption,* Oceana Publications, Inc.: Dobbs Ferry, New York, 1968. Robert A. Farmer, *How to Adopt a Child: A Complete Guide for the Layman,* ARCO Publishing Co.: New York, 1968.

"Bless the beasts and the children, for in this world they have no voice; they have no choice."

—DeVorzon and Botkin